SLEEP LITTLE BABY: THE ROCK-A-BYE BABY SOLUTION FOR MODERN PARENT

Raising a Baby Doesn't Have to Be so Hard! Learn the Best Kept Secrets of Baby Sleep and Enjoy That Long Gone Rested Feeling Again.

Table of Contents

Introduction 5

Chapter 1: A Healthy Sleep Cycle for Your Baby 6

Chapter 2: What Is The Sleep Training Solution? 15

Chapter 3: Babies and Their Sleep Cycles 21

Chapter 4: Why Is Your Baby Crying? 26

Chapter 5: Minimize Sleep Disruptors 36

Chapter 6: How To Use Simple Steps To Help Your Kids Sleep In 48 Hours 44

Chapter 7: Importance Of Establishing A Good Bedtime Routine ... 53

Chapter 8: Sleep Solutions and Strategies 57

Chapter 9: More Health Tips for Mother and Child 65

Chapter 10: Analyze 80

Chapter 11: Teaching Your Baby the Art of Sleeping 85

Chapter 12: Safety 91

Conclusion... 96

Introduction

Whether you are a new parent or a parent-to-be I created this audiobook just for you. I struggled getting my first child to sleep and nap consistently. My husband and I were exhausted and at our wits end. I vowed if I ever found a method, tip or trick that worked I would share it with every parent I knew so that they could experience a good night's rest.

I'm actually the least likely person to be making an audiobook like this as I'm not a doctor and I don't have a professional background. However, I do have a drive and determination to share all I have learned through researching countless articles, books, and blogs, talking with physicians, pediatricians, and several specialists in the field to bring you the tips and techniques in this book.

I have tried to cover a wide range of conditions and "what if" scenarios to give you the best options known to man for helping you and your little one get the rest you need and deserve. Please keep in mind that not every method will work for every child and what worked for the first may not work for the second or third. The important thing to remember is to keep adjusting the techniques you use as your child grows and learns. You are sure to find many practical and proven tips in this handy guide, so jump right in and start learning today so you can get your rest tonight.

Thanks again for purchasing this audiobook, I hope you enjoy it!

Chapter 1: A Healthy Sleep Cycle for Your Baby

What to Expect

After the excitement of a new baby dies down the real work of parenting begins. If you are a new parent then chances are you've been inundated with well-wishers and many with good intentions, each wanting with all their heart to help you. This however, is one of the first tasks you'll have to do as a parent, to sift through all the chaff and come up with a parenting plan that will create a family dynamic that will benefit everyone.

Unfortunately, this is not always easy to do. Just keep in mind that you have three main objectives to accomplish in those first few days with your baby.

1) to get to know your little one. Yes, he or she already has a personality and believe it or not a mind a mind of her own. It is up to you to learn and understand her needs, wants, and expectations.

2) to reinforce the person that is trusting you with their lives. You want your baby to feel safe and cared for. Even at this early stage what you do to reinforce their sense of security can benefit that child for years to come.

3) to enjoy your new role as a parent. There will be times when you will be so exhausted that you won't be able to think straight. There will be times when you won't have a clue what your baby wants. These times can be discouraging, especially when it's 3:00 in the morning and the incessant crying seems to never end but if you use those times to remember the joys of parenthood you'll have a better chance of plowing your way through those rough nights.

The manner in which you and your baby connect can actually influence every aspect of that child's life, not just his or her sleeping patterns so the sooner you decide what type of relationship the two of you will have the sooner the baby will begin to adjust to life in this great big world. This means that you must educate yourself on what a normal baby's sleep patterns should be so you will know when your baby' sleeping schedule is out of whack.

So, what is a normal sleep pattern for a newborn baby? It goes without saying that they will be sleeping a lot. There is a lot of energy expended in being born and the first few days they will be pretty exhausted and in need of rest. According to the babycenter.com, there is nothing unusual about a newborn sleeping as much as 16 to 17 hours a day. The biggest challenge for many parents is that they tend to wake-up at the most inopportune times, at which point their needs must be tended to. This translates into an extremely irregular sleep pattern and a limited amount of sleep for you.

Birth to six weeks: Newborns tend to have unpredictable sleep patterns, which are much shorter than what older children or adults are accustomed to but there is a reason for this. Unlike adults, much of a baby's sleep time is spent in the REM stage (rapid eye movement). This stage is believed to be essential for enhancing the development of their little brains. Still, it can be frustrating when you can't seem to get your REM sleep because your babies REM stage is so short. The good news is that in healthy babies, this stage usually starts to get longer at about six weeks of age.

Six to eight weeks: At around six weeks of age, babies tend to have discerned the difference between day and night. It is at this point that they will naturally begin to adjust their sleep cycles taking shorter naps during the daylight hours and start a longer sleep routine during the night. You can encourage this routine by following some very basic steps in the family routine that will help the baby to understand when it is time to sleep.

Four to six months: At four months, most babies have stretched out their sleeping cycle to at least eight hours and some have managed to sleep through a full twelve hours. While some babies reach this stage earlier (at around two months) most do not reach this milestone until sometime after the four-month marker.

Simple Strategies to Help Babies Learn a Sleeping Schedule

It is important to note that even healthy babies will have trouble slipping into a regular sleeping routine, which can make it very hard for the parents to maintain a consistent schedule. However, there are a few things that can help the baby to acclimate to a more normal sleep cycle. In training your baby to know when to sleep try these simple strategies:

1. In the first few weeks, most babies will only be awake for an hour or two at a stretch. Encourage sleep by making it easy for them to take regular naps. It may seem counterproductive to encourage sleep but if the baby is kept awake for longer than their natural cycle they can become over-stimulated and then it will be more difficult for them to fall asleep naturally.

2. Teach them the difference between night and day. In the daytime keep the room bright and let as much light in as possible. Allow your home to fill with natural noises heard through the day and play and interact with your little one as much as possible. When darkness falls, dim the lights and play soothing music for your baby. The house should be as peaceful as possible and resist the temptation to play with them. This will encourage a more regular sleep pattern and before long the baby will learn to distinguish that daytime is for activity and nighttime for resting on his own.

3. Follow your baby's cues. Babies may not be able to speak but they do know how to let you know when they need something. Look for the different signs they give when they are tired. Watch for the rubbing of the eyes, pulling the ears, and that tell-tale sign of irritability when all their needs are met.

Benefits of Healthy Sleep

Most parents fully expect that in the first few months of a baby's arrival that they are going to lose a lot of sleep. It starts with the feeding times every two or three hours and moves on to answering the baby's cries at all hours throughout the night and day. This routine is perfectly normal in the first few weeks but if you find that your baby is still struggling to sleep through longer stretches of time as they grow older, it is something that needs to be addressed. There are many good reasons why babies need to have good quality sleep in their lives.

You've probably already seen what happens when your baby doesn't get enough sleep. One of the first things you'll notice is that it actually disrupts their attention span, which can have a negative effect on their lives in many ways. Consider these points:

It inhibits their ability to learn. From the time your child enters the world a learning process begins. For your baby's brains to mature they need to be able to sleep well. Studies have shown that those babies that receive higher quality sleep during the night developed better cognitively.

It retards their development. Aside from the impact lack of sleep has on the brain and its ability to learn, prolonged sleep deprivation in your baby could result in other developmental issues. Studies have shown that many children suffering from ADHD did not get enough sleep when they were younger. There is also some concern that this condition could lead to obesity, diabetes, and other serious medical conditions.

With all these things in mind, it is very important that every child no matter what age is able to get an adequate supply of sleep every day. It's is okay to miss a day or two of sleep; it happens to everyone but concern should be that these occasional nights without sleep do not become a pattern that will lead to problems they may have to deal with for the rest of their lives.

What is Healthy Baby Sleep?

Babies are notorious for changing sleep cycles, waking in the night, restlessness, and inconsolable crying. To some, these behaviors may seem erratic or random. However, there are important reasons why your baby sleeps (or doesn't sleep) in the way that she does.

Understanding how baby sleep works is the first step towards giving your baby the healthy sleep she needs for proper development—and to getting back some sleep of your own!

The first question to ask is, what does healthy baby sleep look like?

Healthy baby sleep is more than just getting 'enough' sleep overall, although that is important. Healthy baby sleep also means sleep of the right quality and at the right times. Understanding all that goes into these factors is an enigma to many, but we're here to break it down for you! It all starts by understanding how baby sleep works.

You've no doubt noticed by now that babies change rapidly. As your baby grows, his or her sleep also changes to accommodate development. While every baby is different, there are age-based norms that can help you to understand your baby's changing sleep patterns.

Check out the following table to get an idea of how much sleep your baby needs according to age. Keep in mind that these numbers are averages. Your baby's sleep needs will likely fall within these ranges, but if they seem to need more or less sleep than other babies, it may simply mean that your baby has different sleep needs. If in doubt, speak with your pediatrician.

Keep the following age-specific tips for bedtime:

Newborns

Newborns may go to bed quite late, anywhere from 7pm – 11pm. Their brains have not yet learned to produce melatonin in conjunction with circadian rhythms, so bedtime may not be related to the dark and may not always happen at the same time. Trying to get them to a consistent, early bedtime is good, however, your newborn probably won't be ready for highly structured sleep schedules until closer to 3 months.

3 Months – 18 Months

From 3 months, it's time to start training your baby to have a consistent, early bedtime. We'll be going over some great tips and strategies for sleep training later in this book, but for now, know that you will want to aim for a bedtime around 7pm.

18 Months – 36 Months

As your baby gets older and enters the toddler stage, she will be able to stay up a little later...but not much! Babies in this age range do best with a bedtime between 7 and 8:30.

Don't forget that healthy sleep depends on more than just the amount of sleep your baby gets. Another important factor is your baby's sleep cycles, which reflect the quality of your baby's sleep.

It's not unusual for adults to fall asleep soon after they close their eyes. An adult sleep cycle includes time spent in deep sleep and in REM sleep. The length of the cycle varies depending on whether it is the first, second, or later cycle of the night, but on average lasts between 90 and 120 minutes.

Babies' sleep cycles are similar to adults' in that they involve both deep sleep and REM sleep. However, it takes babies much longer to fall asleep once their eyes are closed. Their cycles are also much shorter, often lasting less than an hour and rarely more than 90 minutes. It's important for your baby to experience complete sleep cycles in order to get the quality of rest they need for proper development.

In addition to quantity and quality of baby sleep, we should also consider timing. Babies don't sleep only at night, and when a baby sleeps plays an important role in preventing tiredness. For babies, daytime sleep is just as important as nighttime sleep.

Newborns sleep often throughout the day and night, and may not exhibit any specific napping pattern. Newborns should be allowed to sleep whenever they need to. Although you can take steps to start developing routines with your newborn, this is not the time to begin hard-core sleep training. Newborns may start to consolidate their napping periods as early as six weeks, and should be ready for more structured sleep training around 3 months.

20 Facts About Baby Sleep

Now that we've gone over the big-picture factors that influence healthy baby sleep, here are 20 important facts that you need to know:

Your baby's clock is off. Most babies don't develop their own circadian rhythms until about 12 weeks old. As a result, melatonin isn't produced in response to darkness the way that it is for you and me. This is one of the reasons that newborn infants sleep on and off around the clock.

Babies like to be close. Many babies find it comforting to sleep close their mothers. This includes both co-sleeping and simply sleeping in the same room as mom. Both have potential advantages for your baby's quality of sleep.

Your soothing could be stimulating. Sometimes a parent's efforts to soothe their baby has the opposite effect. Common examples include wrapping a baby too snuggly in their blanket, talking to them when they're trying to fall asleep, or picking them up every time they make noise in their sleep.

Babies need bedtimes. Routine is helpful for most people, regardless of age, and babies are no different. Babies who are put down for naps around the same time every day tend to fall asleep more easily and wake up less often.

Babies need a change of routine as they grow. The sleep schedule of a newborn will differ from that of a six-month-old or an eight-month-old. Understanding how much sleep babies need at different ages, and how often they need it, will help you to create effective routines for maximizing your baby's healthy sleep.

Babies need to unwind before bed time. Too much stimulus before bed can make it hard for a baby to fall asleep. Choose evening rituals that soothe, rather than stimulate.

Babies like to practice. When babies are learning to sit up, roll over, or crawl, they may wake up in the night to practice these skills. They will often put themselves back to sleep, so avoid further interrupting their sleep by picking babies up unnecessarily.

Babies have short sleep cycles. While the average adult sleep cycle lasts 90-120 minutes, a baby's sleep cycles is usually only 40-60 minutes.

Teething hurts. Babies who are teething wake up more easily due to painful gum irritation.

Babies don't like to be interrupted. Noises and squirming are normal parts of baby sleep; there's usually no need to intervene for these kinds of disruptions.

Your baby is too tired. Overtired babies have a harder time falling asleep and staying asleep. The quality of sleep may also be reduced if your baby is fatigued.

Babies like to suck. Babies are biologically programmed to suck. Providing a breast, bottle, or pacifier will comfort and relax them before and during sleep.

Waking up at night is useful. The ability to wake up easily is an evolutionary advantage that helps babies get their needs taken care of. A poorly sleeping baby can be disheartening, but take comfort in knowing that waking up at night is meant to help keep your baby safe.

Babies need to move. Movement, such as carrying, bouncing, or rocking, can relieve digestive discomfort and muscle pain that keep babies awake.

Closed eyes don't mean deep sleep. Due to their shorter sleep cycles, babies may only be dozing when they appear to be sleeping.

Babies have tiny tummies. Food is processed quickly, and hunger can be painful. Newborn babies need to be fed 8-12 times in every 24 hour period, so they should not sleep through the night.

Babies experience discomfort. Gas, teething, hunger, and thirst are just a few of the common discomforts that babies face. Finding ways to relieve discomfort will help your baby get better sleep.

Babies are learning to self-soothe. Babies don't start out with the skills to soothe themselves. Crying is often the only tool they have to get their needs met. Your baby probably won't begin to learn to self soothe until after three months.

Sleep is important for development. Babies don't just need sleep to get over being tired. Good baby sleep also promotes healthy brain and nervous system development.

Light matters. Sleeping in the dark helps babies' bodies learn to produce melatonin, an important hormone for sleep regulation. Keeping the baby's room dark at night can help them as they develop their own circadian rhythms. On the other hand, having them nap in a dark room during the day may interfere with circadian rhythm, causing babies to wake up more often during the night.

As you can see, baby sleep is affected by a wide variety of factors!

With so many influences, it's no wonder that parents often feel overwhelmed when babies don't sleep well. The more you understand about your baby's sleep needs, the easier it will be to problem solve sleep issues. By taking the time to get a hold on the basics, you will have less stress and a much greater chance for success.

Chapter 2: What Is The Sleep Training Solution?

Sleep training is the way toward helping a baby to figure out alone how to get to sleep and stay asleep during the night.

Some infants do this faster and easier. But many others need help along the way. They have difficulty calming themselves down to sleep, or getting back to sleep when they've awake. In this book, we will try to share the mom's experience. We describe the main approaches to sleep training; we will discuss the existing literature as well as some new developments for 2017.

When can I begin sleep training with my baby?

Most specialists suggest starting when your child is between four and six months old. By around four months, babies have usually begun to build up a healthy sleep-wake cycle and dropped the most of their night feedings. These are signs they might be prepared to start sleep training. Many babies this age are developmentally able to sleep for long intervals during the evening.

Would that be valid in your situation? Your child is unique, and each baby is different. Some babies may not be ready for sleep training until they are older than six months. Some newborn babies sleep more than six or seven hours, while others won't start to do that until later.

You could ask your doctor if you are not sure if your baby is ready for sleep training yet or not.

How to prepare for sleep training - Step by step instructions

Recommendations to set the stage for sleep training successfully:

One of the most important tasks for parents is to have a sleep schedule. In reality, it is never too late to have and stick to the bedtime routine, but the most efficient will be when your baby is around six weeks of age. A part of your routine can be a warm bath and soothing music.

- Timing is relevant for your success as well. You should be very consistent and STICK TO BEDTIME between seven and eight o'clock to avoid children getting over tired.

- Sticking to the predictable daytime schedule is another important factor. Try to get your baby up about the same time every morning. Feed him and put him down for rests at about the same times throughout the day. This routine helps him relax and feel secure, and a happy baby settles down to sleep much more quickly.

- Be sure that your child doesn't have any medical condition that could affect their sleep. It is paramount to address any underlying condition by your doctor.

What are the best sleep training options for me?

Every parent wanders which technique are the best in their situation. You can introduce healthy sleeping habits in many ways. You should understand many of them, and by testing, you should find which one is the most comfortable for you and your child.

You know that what works well for one child, will not necessary work for yours. Get ready to have some trial and error while figuring out an approach suitable for your family and situation.

You can always turn to experts who have written many books on the subject or listen to other parents' experience. Have a look at sleep training basics before you start.

The subject of training children to sleep is written in many books, and you can also find extensive research on the subject. As a result, the conclusions for parents are: "BE CONSISTENT! The training you pick MUST be the one you can stick with and follow through. Be flexible and observe your baby's reaction. If his mood and behavior change for the worse, consider stopping for a few weeks before picking another approach or try the same again."

Baby's Sleep Habits

Babies have different sleep patterns compared to adults. A lot of things can distract them and prevent from going to sleep. There are also lots of things that can disrupt their sleep, especially at night. Also, sleep habits change through the baby's first 12 months of life, making it more difficult to get them got to bed on a regular schedule.

Newborns typically sleep a lot. They sleep on an average of 16 to 17 hours each day. They sleep most of the day and through the night. However, some babies are less inclined to sleep- and stay asleep- for more than 2 to 4 hours during the 1st few weeks after birth. Some wake up frequently, crying and very irritable during the night. Parents lose sleep and become tired and irritable throughout the next day.

Sleep cycles are much shorter in babies compared to adults. Babies have lighter sleep and get disrupted more easily, too. This is because newborns spend more time in a sleep stage called REM (rapid eye movement). The REM stage of sleep is believed to be important during the newborn period and through the rest of infancy because it supports rapid brain development.

When the baby is 6 to 8 weeks old, sleep during the day is often reduced to short naps and nighttime sleep generally lasts longer at this age. Most babies would wake up night only to feed. REM stage is also shortened. Babies at this age generally spend longer periods in the non-REM stage of sleep, which is deeper and less easily disturbed.

At 3 months of age, babies sleep on an average of 15 hours. This includes both daytime naps and nighttime sleep.

By 4 to 6 months, babies generally are able to sleep through the night for 8 to 12 hours. Some babies reach this milestone in as early as 6 weeks old, but most do so by 5 months of age.

At 4 months of age, babies typically have started to adapt a fairly regular pattern of sleeping and waking hours. There is reduced waking up during the night for their nighttime feedings. Even with the sleep-wake pattern, this is not the time to impose rigid sleeping programs. The baby's pattern at this point would have been an adjustment to family life. The sleep/wake pattern is more likely in response to the general schedule of activities within the home.

What parents can do when the baby has started to display sleep/wake patterns is to try sleep training. Learn a few sleep training methods that can be used for this age. Observe how the baby reacts to the method and adjust accordingly. Parents should not force the baby to stick to a chosen method. Instead, parents should adjust their methods depending on the baby's response. Every baby responds in a unique way when it comes to sleep. If the baby shows any indication that he is not yet ready for sleep training, take a step back. Let the baby follow his own sleep patterns and techniques, then try sleep training again after a few weeks.

Between the ages of 4 to 6 months, most babies are now able to sleep through the night. Waking up for nighttime feedings becomes less frequently as the baby grows older. Sleeping through the night now means sleeping 8 to 12 hours straight, without waking up for feedings or need for a diaper change. This is good news for parents, as they get more sleep at night, too.

Some babies, however, are still unable to sleep for 8 hours straight. A lot of babies still have to wake up frequently for nighttime feedings. This is normal. Remember that babies have their own unique sleeping patterns and reach certain milestones at different rates.

It is also normal for babies who have been regularly sleeping through the night to return to waking up frequently again. This does not indicate that something is wrong. More likely, the baby is becoming more socially aware. The baby waking up is more because of the need for the parents' company.

How to Establish Good Sleep Habits

Establishing good sleeping habits should start as early as possible. It does not mean training the baby at a very young age. Establishing good sleep habits means promoting a consistent sleep schedule and helping the baby associate sleep as a secure, comforting and desirable activity.

Recognizing signs

Parents should be aware of the signs that the baby is sleepy and cater to the need in a timely manner. Waiting too long before putting the baby to sleep will make him too tired and sleep will be more difficult. They should act on these signs immediately by promoting an environment conducive for sleep.

A few common signs that the baby is ready for sleep include:

- rubs or brings his hands over his eyes
- flicks or brings his hand to his ear
- appearance of faint, dark circles under the baby's eyes
- becomes more fussy than usual
- Easily irritated- baby cries and whines at the slightest provocation
- blankly stares into space
- Frequently stretches and yawns
- loses interest in his environment, such as in people and toys, and turns away
- Increasingly turns quiet and lies still
- Buries face into the parent's (or caregiver's) chest

Teaching day and night

As early as 2 weeks old, parent can start teaching babies to differentiate day from night. Associate different activities for day and night. For example, during the day, keep the room bright. Interact with the baby a lot, such as talking and playing more often. Let the baby hear regular daytime household noise such as music, phones and sounds of household appliances running like TVs and dishwashers. Wake him up if he tends to fall asleep during his daytime feedings. At night, spend less time with active play. Start to minimize household noise. Turn down music or the TV. Also, turn the lights down low. Over time, the baby will figure out that active play and noisy environments are for daytime. Low lights and quiet environments will denote "night" and a transition time for sleep.

Start a bedtime routine

Babies learn by association and through repeated experiences. Take advantage of this by initiating bedtime rituals. Baths, changing clothes, and lullabies are simple ways to start a bedtime routine.

Chapter 3: Babies and Their Sleep Cycles

It is an undeniable fact that having a newborn in the house can wreak havoc on the sleep patterns and schedules of new parents. Staying awake may lead to increased crankiness, but it generally has little long-term health effects. Babies are like little snowflakes, every one of them has different traits that may affect how much physical activity they like, how long they sleep at night, and how much they cry as a whole. Typical babies are usually quite self-soothing; they have a schedule for sleeping and feeding and usually fall asleep on their own. However, do not be quick to blame yourself or feel discouraged if you have an atypical baby who is less self-soothing. As a parent, there are many things you can do and many methods you can try to help your little angel sleep better at night.

States and Stages of Sleep

Babies' sleep patterns change as they age. Though the stages of sleep are pretty basic, actually getting a child to sleep may require certain adjustments and foresight. While many veteran parents may already know this, sometimes a refresher is needed. Additionally, first-time parents and parents adopting either their first child or a child of a different age than their other children should find the following information very useful as it is sorted by age. In the beginning, a lot of observation is required. Despite this, you can start setting up a schedule and adjust your plan as your child's needs change. So let's take a closer look at sleep regulation and how it affects both babies and adults.

For most, sleep is regulated by outward stimuli (i.e. light and dark surroundings, noise levels, etc.) The circadian biological clock rhythms have not yet been developed at any level for children less than 6 months old. For adults, the internal circadian rhythm can be affected by whether or not they are a morning or evening person, so consider yourself as well when attempting to identify your child's sleep habits. Many people argue strongly for genetics and the nature versus nurture argument, so it is worth mentioning that if you are an evening person, then either by genetics or by your own habits rubbing off on your child, you may start to notice that your child has likes and dislikes similar to your own when it comes to sleeping.

Not only does the body's internal circadian biological clock regulate sleeping patterns, but there is also the additional involvement of sleep/wake homeostasis. Your internal circadian biological clock responds to signals sent throughout the body by a group of cells in the hypothalamus gland called the suprachiasmatic nucleus (SCN). Once these cells respond to the surrounding dark or light received through the optic nerve in the eyes, they signal other parts of the brain to start waking you up or making you feel sleepy. When there is light and the other parts of the brain are signaled to wake you, cortisol and other hormone levels are raised, melatonin and similar hormones are lowered, and the temperature of your body rises. It is the opposite when it is dark and you are going to sleep. These are the settings you want your baby to have in the future.

Next, we will take a closer look at how children sleep according to age.

Newborns (1-2 months old)

Sleep is the main activity for a newborn, followed closely by feedings and diaper changes. On average, a newborn sleeps between 11 and 18 hours a day when all the time is added up. The clock governing your infant's sleep-wake times is set by need. While asleep, their faces, arms, and legs may twitch; they may smile, attempt to suck their fists or thumbs, and may generally be a bit wiggly even while they sleep. When it is time for a nap, babies will express their need for rest in many ways. And with a bit of extended observation, you too can learn your baby's indicators.

Fussing, yawning, crying, and rubbing their eyes are classic sleepy indicators. For the best results, it is best to put your baby to bed when they display signs of sleepiness rather than putting them to bed after they have already fallen asleep in your arms. This directly ties into self-soothing, which tends to be easier when your baby is close enough to sleep. By putting a newborn to bed when they are extremely sleepy — as opposed to when they are already asleep — your baby will fall asleep quicker and much more reliably.

Furthermore, a newborn will nap at intervals throughout the day, regardless, but by exposing them to more light, sound, and playful attention during the day, their bodies will begin to associate the dimmer, quieter environment of the evening with the reduction in activity. These steps are the groundwork that encourage more nighttime sleep and more restful nights for all.

In brief then, the best tip for starting sleep training with your newborn is to simply observe signs of sleepiness which will allow you to put your baby in their crib before they actually fall asleep. Lay your baby on their back to sleep without any blankets, pillows, or soft items near their head. And once again, encourage your baby to sleep more at night by exposing them to more activity, light, and sounds during the day and by significantly reducing those things during the night at established times.

Infants (3-11 months old)

Between the ages of 3 and 11 months, your infant's nighttime feeding requirements should begin to taper off. By 4 months, your baby should be able to sleep for at least 4 to 5 hours straight. And in most cases, nighttime feedings are no longer a necessity by 6 months of age. At this age, your baby should be sleeping throughout the night as well as napping 1 to 4 times a day, with an average time that ranges between 30 minutes long for more frequent naps and 2 hours long during minimal naps. There are keys to maintaining this successfully. Infants typically need 9 to 12 hours' worth of sleep per night.

Once again, place your baby in their crib when they show that they are sleepy rather than after they fall asleep for both naps and bedtime. Be sure to keep their bedding area friendly and stable, and get a good night light that gives off just the right amount of dim light to see but not enough to keep the baby awake — and be sure to keep it in the same spot. Also, place the baby monitor in an ideal location as opposed to moving it around too often. Remember, consistent stability is key.

Be wary of accidentally setting up inhibiting routines like always rocking your baby to sleep. A standard bedtime routine would typically include dinner, a bath, placing the baby in a comfortable sleeper, and then putting him or her to bed. It is incredibly important that your baby learn to self-soothe. A baby with a standard sleeping schedule who is a self-soother will make it easier to pinpoint irregularities and find out whether something is wrong. If your baby is usually asleep at a particular time and starts to fidget or becomes increasingly uncomfortable, it can be easier to pinpoint social, developmental, or health concerns. When babies feel ill, they are more likely to experience disrupted sleep. Now is the perfect time to establish a regular bedtime routine if you have not already done so. And for those of you who have, just keep at it. It is the best way to go.

Toddlers (1-3 years old)

Overall, toddlers need an average of 13 hours of sleep per day. When your baby reaches 18 months, they should be down to one nap that lasts between 1 to 3 hours long. It is important that this nap be taken early in the afternoon to avoid any issues with bedtime. At this age, toddlers may begin to resist going to bed. They may have nightmares or wake up and fight not to go back to sleep. And the fact that they can now get up and walk around as they please also makes it more difficult to keep them in bed.

Thus, during this stage, it is incredibly important to maintain the sleep schedule as rigorously as possible. The bedtime schedule can now include a soothing song or story. Keep the layout and design of the bedroom that your toddler sleeps in the same each night. The inclusion of a security object, like a special stuffed animal or blanket, can make a big difference in keeping your toddler in bed as well. Enforce the bedtime routine nightly, and if it should become necessary, add in an early daytime nap schedule to aid your toddler in being tired by bedtime.

Differentiating Between Sleepy Signs and Fatigue Signs

Knowing when to take a newborn to their crib becomes easier once you familiarize yourself with specific baby sleep signs. When you see your baby yawning, rubbing their eyes, or fussing, it is time to take them to their crib — the ultimate place for them to sleep. Other signs include decreased activity, being less vocal, being quieter, displaying slower motions, and eyelids drooping.

However, sometimes you may think that your baby needs sleep and so you take them to their crib only to find out that they will not go to sleep. This usually happens when parents misinterpret the signs of fatigue for sleep signals. Your little one is fatigued if you see him or her rubbing their eyes, fussing and being cranky, or becoming overtired. This is not the time to take them to their crib, but it requires taking other measures first. However, if the initial efforts aren't bearing any fruit, it is time to look for a more sophisticated and effective method to help your baby be a self-soother. They really need your help here.

Chapter 4: Why Is Your Baby Crying?

Babies are adorable little creatures. They are stress-relievers. When you're exhausted from work and you see your baby smile, it takes away all your fatigue. What a baby does is bring colors to your world. Suddenly, life has meaning. She is your reason for living. Although it can be blissful raising a baby, it is tedious to put them to sleep. Many parents struggle with it. If you have a baby who cries a lot and finds it extremely hard to fall asleep, you may want to find out why. You would be able to resolve the problem once you understand why your baby is crying. This list will help you find out the reason why your baby cries.

Your baby may be hungry. Hunger is almost always the culprit why a baby cries. That's how she communicates that she wants to be fed. Try to remember the last time you fed her milk and if it's about time to feed her again. Watch out for other signs like a baby sucking her finger. That's a sure sign your baby is hungry.

Your baby wants to sleep. Another reason why babies cry is simply because they want to sleep and they aren't comfortable with their position. Some babies sleep when their mothers carry them. Some sleep with a background music on. It is different for every baby. Once you figure this out, your life becomes easier.

Your baby doesn't want a dirty diaper. Perhaps she has been wearing it for hours and it needs to be changed. Or your baby may have pooped on her diaper. Sometimes the only solution is to change. Once you do, your baby will usually stop crying.

Your baby wants you to carry her. Perhaps the reason your baby is crying is she wants you to hold her. Babies are very attached to their mothers. They can even recognize their scent. If after you hold her she stops crying, try to cuddle her or put her to sleep.

Your baby may be sick. If your baby cries for hours and doesn't stop, especially after feeding her, you may want to see a doctor. Perhaps she is having problems with her tummy.

Teething. If your baby is between 4-7 months old, you may want to check her gums. At this age, babies usually get teeth already and it's painful.

Your baby just feels like crying. This is very normal. There are babies who cry for no reason at all. If your baby cries persistently for at least three hours, she may have colic. This crying condition is normal for a healthy baby. This usually occurs when your baby is about 2 weeks old, but it goes away after four months.

How to find out what he's crying about

For a first-time mom, it might be a little difficult to find out why your baby is crying. As you spend more time with your little one, you tend to recognize patterns and certain behaviors that allow you to determine the reason why your baby is crying. You could also check this list.

You may have noticed that newborns have a very high-pitched voice. This doesn't always mean that your baby is in pain. That's just how babies cry.

You will notice a baby is hungry when he fusses and squirms. When this happens, feed your baby right away.

If your baby is in pain, you will have a hard time consoling him. You will also see it in your baby's face that he's in pain.

How to Soothe a Crying baby

Consoling a crying baby is one of the most challenging jobs of a parent, but we are offering some of the gentle ways to soothe your crying baby. The first thing you should do when your baby starts crying is take a long deep breath and go with the basics. Feed your baby and change her diapers. Sometimes this will do the trick. If this doesn't work, just stay calm and try these tips:

Rock-a bye baby. Gently hold your baby in your arms and swivel back and forth. This often works but try not to overdo it. When you keep doing this every single time your baby cries, she becomes dependent.

Go with a soothing sound. Sometimes noises make a baby cry. Experiment with different background music and see which will work for your baby. You may want to sing to her as well. Sometimes she responds more to that.

Get your baby outside. They like looking at things especially colorful things. A change of scenery may calm and stop her from crying.

Get a swing for your baby. Movements help calm the baby. Create one specifically designed for your infant or toddler. Again, don't overdo this else your baby becomes dependent on the swing. She might not be able to fall asleep without it.

Try the 5 S's. The 5S are Swinging, Swaddling, Sucking, Side soothing, and using Sshhing sounds. Wrap your baby in a blanket or hold him on his side. You may also want to give your baby a pacifier.

Give your baby a soothing massage.

Check if the temperature inside your house is either too warm or too cold for the baby.

You may also want to check your baby's clothes. Perhaps they are too tight and she needs to change it. Always use loose clothes for your baby. They sleep better with those.

Talk to her gently. A baby listens to the mother. One of the most effective ways to soothe a baby is to talk to her quietly. Assure her that you will always be there for her.

Distract your baby with a toy.

Carry your baby. That makes her feel safe and secure.

Sometimes bathing can do wonders for the baby. Try giving your baby a warm bath before bedtime.

Try all the strategies mentioned above and see which one works for your baby and keep doing it.

How to Soothe a Crying Toddler

Do not tolerate negative behavior. It is best to start disciplining your child early. If your baby demands something you cannot give and he starts to cry, do not give in. Try not to let your anger set in as well. Be gentle with your child and refuse.

Give him something to do. A toddler likes to play during the day. Take him to a playgroup or any trips where there are other kids. This will surely make him tear-free.

There are times when you need to give in. If your toddler wants something, reconsider. Do not say no right away. If it doesn't harm him or your budget, say yes. That will surely stop his tears.

Gentle Ways to Put your Baby to Sleep

You may have tried all the ways of putting your baby to sleep, and they don't seem to work. Everyday, you keep losing sleep because your baby is awake when it's time for you to sleep. If you are a first-time mom, you may want to recognize sleeping signs from your baby first so you would know if he is ready to sleep or not. You need to spot signs if your baby is already tired. Look for these signs from your baby:

The baby rubs his eyes and tries to cry

The baby suddenly loses in interest in whatever he's doing. When he's playing with his toys, he throws it away

If you're carrying him, he may suddenly bury his face in your chest.

The baby suddenly becomes quiet

These signs are telling you that it's time to put the baby to sleep. Put him down on his cot and let him take his nap. As much as possible, avoid eye contact with your baby when you're trying to put him to sleep. That would only encourage the baby to snap out of him sleep zone.

When you see any of these signs, quietly put your baby to bed.

How to teach your baby to sleep soundly?

Babies do not yet know how sleeping works. As a parent, it is essential for you to teach your baby or toddler how and when to sleep. Following a routine is very helpful. As soon as your baby wakes up in the morning, open the curtains to allow sunlight to set into your home. This would let the baby know that it is time to wake up.

Do this every morning until the baby gets used to it. You may want to have background music on, something lively like nursery rhymes. When you have bathed and fed him, play with your baby. You should only play with your baby during the day.

At night, dim all lights and put some soothing music on. Prepare your baby for bed about two hours before bedtime. You may read him a book. Do not expose your baby to bright lights so he would know the difference between day and night.

If the baby tries to cry after putting him down, just pat the baby gently. Tell him it's okay because you're around. You may lie down together and cuddle her. Try to pretend you're also asleep so he knows it's really time to go to bed. Avoid carrying your baby while putting him to sleep. He becomes dependent on it over time.

You could also try these other tips:

Allow your baby to sleep on his own between six to eight months. This will make him not dependent on you all the time. When you see signs that the baby is already sleepy, gently put the baby to sleep. If she cries, pat her gently.

Try massaging your baby before sleeping. Before doing this, make sure the room is pleasant and comfortable to set the right mood. The massage should last not more than 15 minutes.

Give the baby a security object like a clean stuffed animal or a fresh baby blanket. For breastfeeding moms, try putting some breast milk on a piece of fabric and put it beside your baby. Since babies have strong sense of smell, the smell of the fabric may calm her.

Always attend to your baby's needs. If she wakes up crying in the night, find out why. Check her diapers as it might be full. Or your baby could be hungry.

Don't allow your baby to stay up too late. If he is still awake at 9pm, you might want to check his nap schedule. Schedule it in the early afternoon, not a couple of hours before bedtime.

When you feed him during the night, stay quiet. Avoid chatting with your baby so he knows it's time for bed.

Sleep problems and solutions for babies:

Problem: Your baby is awake at night and asleep during the day.

This means the baby still isn't aware that nighttime is for sleeping. To help your baby sleep, take her outside during the day. Socialize and play with her. Be active. You could take a walk in the park with your baby. Inside the house, allow plenty of sunlight to get in. Play some active music. Watch less television. At sundown, dim the lights and turn off television. Music should be soothing. Avoid a lot of talk with the baby to encourage him to sleep.

Problem: The baby wakes up in the middle of the night.

Do not turn on the lights when your baby wakes up. This shift might tell her brain it's time to wake up. What you can do is carry the baby for a few minutes then put the baby back in the bed. Wait for a few minutes until he is settled in, then leave the room quietly.

Ways to Put your Toddlers to Sleep

Toddlers need adequate sleep every night for their emotional and cognitive development. But they're very active and don't seem to want to go to sleep. When they're very tired and sleepy, they fight it. And they never get tired of playing. If you have a very challenging toddler, try these tips:

Help him set his biological clock. Set a time for sleeping every night. If possible, let him prepare for bed early, say about 7 pm. Avoid letting him sleep late or when he's very tired. When a toddler is exhausted, his adrenalin and cortisol levels kick in. This would only keep him going. When this happens, toddlers find it harder to sleep during the night, and they wake up too soon. Dim the lights so he knows it's time to sleep. Avoid bright lights in his bedroom. Make him comfortable. His bed should be cozy. You may want to have a clean stuffed animal beside him to let him sleep right away.

Prepare a bedtime light snack for your toddler. Some toddlers prefer to eat before sleeping. While reading him stories, let him have a healthy snack and try something without sugar.

Get him sunlight and fresh air during the day. Let them play and socialize with other kids. Toddlers tend to sleep soundly during the night when they are active during the day. Just don't let them play a few hours before bedtime. It might just re-energize them. If you're good with humor, make your toddlers laugh. It's good for them.

Acknowledge your toddler's courage if he tries to sleep on his own. Talk to your toddler about sleeping alone and give him prizes in the morning if he doesn't cry or looks for you in his bed. Practicing motivation is good for the toddler. You can give him perhaps a new toy when you go out or food in the morning. Something he really likes to eat.

If a toddler is afraid to sleep in the dark, try telling him cheerful stories before bedtime. If he wakes up from a scary dream assure him it's gone now and that you're always there for him. Never tell him it's not real as dreams may seem very real to them. Just tell your toddler there is no need to worry.

Sleep problems and solutions for toddlers

Problem: Your toddler keeps getting in and out of bed.

If your toddler is already on his bed, but he keeps getting out, the reason is he doesn't want to go to sleep yet. You might want to try to do something creative with him. Try reading or listening to some relaxing music. You could also talk to him about a story you've read. If this doesn't work out, ask him what he needs. If he wants to get out of bed, let him. It's okay to sometimes make the child feels he is in control so long as you don't do it often.

Problem: Your child is already in bed for hours and he still can't sleep.

The one reason children can't sleep right away is because they have been playing or taking naps perhaps 1 or 2 hours before bedtime. Make sure naps are in the morning or early afternoon. Also, do not let your child play when it's almost bedtime.

Developing good sleeping practices with your baby or child

Sleeping is important to everyone's well-being and growth. For children, it makes them feel refreshed and alive during the day. They are unlikely to be irritable if they have a good night's sleep. Children remain alert and sharp when they are well rested. To help your child develop good sleeping habits, try these tips.

Try to minimize bedtime rituals. You may not completely eliminate this but being with your baby every time he is about to go to bed would make him dependent on you. You can still nurse or sing to him at bedtime but make sure you place him in his bed when he is still awake. It is better if he gets used to his mattress so in case he wakes up, he will not look for you.

Don't let your baby fall asleep with his bottle. If he gets used to it, he will depend on it as well. He will not be able to sleep without the bottle. The extra calories may also interfere with his body rhythms and might wake him up when his hungry or milk might pool on the baby's ear and will cause an infection. To avoid these, make sure you won't let him accustomed to have his bottle before bedtime.

Don't sleep with your baby beside you. Helping your baby sleep on his own would make him become independent. It would also reduce anxiety. If he's already used to it, try to eliminate it slowly until he gets used to sleeping alone.

Help him overcome his fear of being separated from you. At six months, your baby might feel abandoned if you're not with him when he sleeps. To avoid this, try to spend time with your baby about 15 minutes before he goes to bed. When he's already in his crib, talk for about five minutes and gently touch him. Then leave the room quietly.

Dealing with sleep problems

Bed-wetting

This is normal for younger children. This becomes a problem when the child is more than five years old and he still wets his bed at least twice a week. The best thing to do is let your child know it is a normal condition and that it is a no big deal.

You should also tell the other family members to not tease your child if he wet his bed. To help eliminate this problem, you need to monitor your toddler's fluid intake. You could also try waking him up after a few hours. If this doesn't help, try to talk to your pediatrician. He might be able to give you other options to help your child overcome this problem.

Sleep Deprivation

When your child isn't getting enough sleep, he will have trouble concentrating. He may perform poorly in school too. There are things you can do to find out if your child isn't getting enough sleep.

Observe if your child falls asleep when inside the car.

He doesn't wake up early in the morning.

You will notice that your child is overly sensitive and very irritable.

He sleeps way early than his usual bedtime.

If you see these signs, try to adjust his routines for him to have quality sleep every night.

Colic and How to Remedy it

One of the challenges of being a parent is when a baby cries for hours for no reason. Colic is a condition where babies less than 4 months old cries for about 3 hours a day and 3 days a week. This happens to healthy babies, and it can be really stressful for a parent, but don't worry as it goes away after 3 or 4 months.

The cause of this condition is unknown. There was research done about colic, but they still couldn't figure out why it happens to healthy babies. Some of its symptoms include:

Crying episodes happen the same day every day for a few minutes to up to three hours. What a parent should do when this happens: Check your baby after crying as he might pass gas after a colic episode.

Intense crying. Colic is mysterious. No one really knows why it happens. When your baby cries, he is inconsolable. Nothing will make him stop crying.

Crying for no reason. When your baby has colic, he cries for no reason at all and you might notice some changes in the baby. He might clench his fists during a colic episode.

Some babies do not have Colic. Mothers who smoke before and after pregnancy contributes to an infant's colic.

Breastfed infants and first-borns are also not prone to colic. Colic disappears after 3 or 4 months. If it doesn't and you've tried doing everything to soothe your baby, talk to your pediatrician.

Here's what you can do before you make that appointment: Track how many times your baby cries and how many minutes or hours. Then write down how you've tried soothing your baby. You may list down other questions you have for the pediatrician.

Tips for soothing your baby:

Hold your baby gently during a colic episode. Hold them upright to prevent them to swallow air.

Have your baby burp after feeding.

Bath and massage your baby. This is very helpful and may calm the baby.

Chapter 5: Minimize Sleep Disruptors

Quite often, what deprives children of quality sleep aren't the conditions present during sleeping time but what they do shortly before it. In particular, the food and drinks children eat and drink, respectively, as well as children's activities shortly before bedtime can result in shallow and easily disrupted sleep. These include:

Food Intake: Do not feed your child food and drinks that are chock full of sugar because it'll make the child hyperactive just before bedtime, which will definitely make it hard for a child to sleep.

Extra-Curricular: Don't play with your child or do other activities with him – such as watching TV or playing video games on the tablet or on your smartphone – that are stimulating because it will make your child too stimulated to fall asleep early.

Errands: Avoid working your child's sleeping time around the errands you need to do or your other family activities. Do the opposite instead – work these activities around your child's sleep time. This will allow your toddler to get much needed quality snooze time on a regular basis.

Lighting: Use soft lights in the toddler's room at night as the child winds down to sleep because bright lights hinder the production of the sleep hormone melatonin, which will make it harder to fall asleep at night. When the child is about to sleep, turn off the lights or if he/she is uncomfortable in total darkness, keep a small lamp on that will give enough soft light to appease your child enough to be able to go to sleep. This will help keep the room just dark enough to be conducive to sleeping.

Sleeping Cues

It will be too late if you only put your child to sleep when he's already acting tired. The best time to put him to bed is when he starts exhibiting sleeping cues and not when already exhausted. What do these cues look like?

In general, they include him being cranky, unable to focus his attention on anything, yawning and eye-rubbing. Observe your child carefully to discover what his unique sleeping cues are so that you won't miss them when they happen. Failure to catch those cues and act accordingly can make it much harder for him to go to sleep as, by then, he will already be frantic, jumpy, or wired.

The Importance of Consistency

To help your child sleep well easily at night, you need to make the child feel a sense of inevitability, safety and calmness. And these can be accomplished by establishing a regular routine that may involve taking a nice warm bath, bedtime story reading, kissing, prayers or blessings and bed tucking right before turning off the lights for sleep. With bedtime routines, it's important not to overdo them. Doing so may take up excess time and make your child miss his sleeping windows of opportunity and have a hard time sleeping afterward.

What if your child becomes resistant or stubborn with the routine and chooses not to go with the flow? Just try to make the clock the bad guy, instead of you! How? One way to do this is by making your child a simple chart of the steps involved in the bedtime routine, which you can post in this child's room. Each step on the chart should feature a picture of your child doing each step and a clock's time that corresponds to the time at which each of the activities must be accomplished. As you go through the bedtime routine you want to establish every night with your child, point to the relevant photos. In time, your child will gradually want to cooperate.

An even better way to do this is by giving him an incentive. You can say something like:

"Hey, it's 7:00 already! You know what? We can have an extra story to read later, just before lights out, if you finish brushing your teeth now."

That should give your child the opportunity to see you as his ally rather than a stern drill sergeant. More than that, it allows him to develop a good sense of personal responsibility and the ability to make wise choices later on.

Wind Down Early

Don't expect an easy time putting your child to bed if you abruptly stop his activities and expect him to go cold turkey! Your child needs enough time to wind down, relax and be in the mood to hit the sack. To allow for this, give your child an hour or two of quiet and calmness in order to slowly wind down into a relaxed state of mind and body that's conducive to deep and restful sleep throughout the night.

A Comfortable Sleeping Environment

As part of their normal sleep cycles, it's normal for toddlers to wake up slightly in the middle of their sleep. They usually return to a deep state of slumber relatively quickly. As a parent, what you must concern yourself with is that they don't fully wake up during those "semi" wake up moments in the middle of the night due to a feeling or sense of discomfort. To ensure this doesn't happen, it will be worth investing in a bed or mattress that makes your child sleep comfortably through those minor sleep-waking moments.

Another factor that determines how comfortable your child's sleeping environment can be is room temperature. A room that's too hot or too cold can make it uncomfortable enough to disrupt your child's sleep. During the summer months, a breezy or air-conditioned room can help your child sleep comfortably while a warm pair of PJs and nice warm blanket can make it comfortable for him to sleep during the icy months of the year.

Another factor that influences your child's ability to sleep comfortably is lighting – or lack of it. Light makes people feel awake and makes it hard for them to sleep so it's best to use soft lights in your child's room especially during the last hour or two before sleeping, as I mentioned earlier. It will also help if you make his room as dark as is comfortably possible when he's already sleeping. Light makes it hard for your child's body to produce melatonin, which is a key sleeping hormone. So keep the lights down…or off.

The Biological Clock

If you want your toddler to sleep well, his body must learn how to anticipate or expect sleep at a specific time in the evening. For most toddlers, going to sleep between 6:30 p.m. and 8:00 p.m. is the ideal.

While it may be tempting to think that sleeping later in the evening will tire your child out and make him fall asleep more easily, it won't. When he stays up late, stress hormones such as cortisol and adrenalin start kicking in due to being over-tired, which will make him do as the Energizer bunny does… keep going and going and going and going. By then, it'll be much harder for him to sleep at night. After that, you'll have a hard time sleeping due to the stress.

And when he has a hard time falling asleep, guess what? He'll wake up more frequently throughout the night and will tend to wake up earlier in the day. When that happens, expect a cranky toddler during the day. Just continue experimenting with different sleeping times until you're able to see which time is optimal in terms of minimizing or keeping your child from being all wound up.

Another way to establish a consistent sleeping routine is turning by down the lights at least one hour prior to going to bed. Coupled with calm and slow routines, it helps program your child's body and mind to anticipate falling asleep at a certain time in the evening. A consistent, slow and calm pre-sleeping routine is a very effective way to lull your child to sleep compared to one that's abrupt, such as simply putting him in pajamas and turning off the lights within 2 minutes.

The key sleeping cue to watch out for here (remember our discussion on sleeping cues?) is him starting to becoming sleepy. Once you continue letting him stay awake past this moment, his body will switch to overdrive and stimulate him with adrenaline to the point when it will be very hard, if not downright impossible, to lull him into a deep and restful sleep soon.

Don't Deny the Naps Too Soon

Most toddlers are neither emotionally nor physiologically prepared to give up their regular naps – at least not until they turn 3 years old. Thus, you might consider taking it easy on your child if he still wants to take naps throughout the day before the age of 3. If you deny the toddler that, both of you will pay a heftier price in the evening – and the following day – when your child becomes too adrenalized and cranky to sleep early.

Midnight Snacks

Particularly during those growth spurt years, toddlers need to eat midway into the night. Some of the best choices for midnight snacks that won't disrupt their sleep are calming and predictable food and drinks such as a piece of toast, a slice of turkey and a glass of warm milk. The key is to choose food and drinks that are neither stimulating nor loaded with sugar. You can move your child much better through your pre-sleep routine if you can make the child eat a snack at a table in the child's room as you read them their bedtime stories. Just make sure he brushes his teeth afterward, just before going to sleep.

If your toddler still tends to still fall asleep with a feeding bottle in hand and mouth, you should disassociate him from it. Doing so will enable him to easily go back to sleep during those slight waking moments in the middle of the night because he won't be stimulated into waking up completely as he drinks from the bottle.

Regular Exercise, Laughter, and the Great Outdoors

It turns out the old folks are right when they say that for kids to sleep more soundly at night, they need to play outdoors as much as possible and not just sit inside the house playing computer games or watching TV all the time. This is great for your child too for as long as it's not a few hours before bedtime, as it will just make your toddler too energized in the evening to the point of having a difficult time sleeping.

It's also important that your child gets to laugh often because doing so allows him to bring down his stress hormone levels. Kids who normally have a hard time falling and staying asleep at night are those that carry a lot of emotional baggage. Laughing heartily and frequently can help your toddler unload emotional baggage (if he has any) to fall deeply asleep at night.

Develop New Habits for Sleeping

You may be doing your child a disservice if you're always rocking or nursing him to sleep. Why? You're making him get used to always being with you while asleep. This may result in him always looking for you as his security blanket in order to be able to go back to sleep during those mini waking times throughout the night. And that's part of his normal sleep cycle. When you're not there, going back to sleep will be very hard or practically impossible.

Your child's pre-sleep routine may not necessarily involve rocking or nursing the toddler to sleep but may nevertheless make it hard for him to go back to sleep on his own when he wakes up slightly in the middle of the night. Thus, it's important that you help him develop new sleeping habits that will empower him to sleep soundly on his own.

It may be hard at first so it's best to do this one step at a time. For example, instead of going cold turkey and just stopping rocking him to sleep, you can start by rocking him for shorter periods of time until you completely stop doing so. It'll be very difficult to develop new sleeping habits by simply going cold turkey on the one you want to replace. It must be done, pardon the pun, in baby steps.

Don't Rush It

Speaking of establishing new and independent sleeping habits, start by holding him while he goes off to sleep but not in a lying position because that puts you at risk of falling asleep as well! To help you to relax and make the most of this bonding moment, just meditate or listen to soft music.

Once your child is accustomed to falling asleep as you hold him, you should start making him accustomed to falling asleep by simply holding his hand or placing your hand on his head or forehead. You can also choose to substitute this by using a big stuffed toy or pillow in your place. Kids often love cuddling and curling around a nice, soft stuffed animal or a pillow, although it is important to choose a toy that is safe.

When your child is already able to fall asleep simply by being touched and not held, try sitting beside your child while he falls asleep. At first, you'll need to sit really close so that your child can touch you easily when he reaches out to you.

The last frontier is when your child's able to fall asleep without any physical contact with you. You then start to move your seat slowly further and further away from your child until you're able to exit the room. In moments that your child wakes up and tries to sit up, just say, "Lie down now please…it's sleep time, it's bed time." in a monotone voice.

You can also try and do something around the room while your child falls asleep. Just make sure what you'll be doing isn't noisy or will in any way distract your child from his sleep. Doing this will give your sleeping child a sense of security with your presence in the room and your proximity. You can then begin staying outside your child's room for longer and longer periods of time until you're able to finally help your child develop the habit of sleeping independently.

On those days that your child backslides and needs your physical touch again, don't sweat it. It won't derail the overall progress for as long as it doesn't happen frequently and consecutively. Just keep at it and the independent sleeping habit will eventually be established.

Lying Down with the Child on the Adult Bed

It's easy for most toddlers, yours included probably, when parents lie down with them on their beds. This can be especially challenging for the parents because often times, they themselves fall asleep and would have to wake up just to go their own rooms, at which point their sleep's already disrupted. Their evening sleep's practically ruined by then. It also makes the child dependent on the presence of the parents to fall and stay asleep, which is a behavior that actually needs to be corrected.

That's why some parents choose to let their toddler or baby sleep in their own bed until they're old enough to sleep on their own. It minimizes the disruption in their sleep. And most kids are able to adjust well to sleeping in their own beds and rooms as they reach a certain age so this strategy is one that many parents have adopted.

There's no right or wrong between the two. As the parent of your toddler, you're in the best position to see which option is best for your child, especially when it comes to helping him get deep and restful sleep.

Let Your Child Know What Will Happen

For this, you can do something fun. Pretend to act out a mini-play using props such as your child's stuffed toys and if none are available, use his pillows. Here, one of the "characters" will play the part of putting off bedtime. Using the props, act out what will actually happen as part of the pre-sleep routine.

For example, you act out the part of the "parents" by saying "It's bed time!" Then, you can act out the baby's role (represented by one of the props) asking to be cuddled or rocked to sleep in reaction to the call to go to bed. Next, you also act out the parents' response to the request where they say "No, we will just hold you as you go to bed." Then, you can act out the part where the baby prop cries, to which the parents respond by holding the child until he eventually settles down and sleeps.

When acting out the firmness part of the skit, it's important to do so in a calm and loving manner that firmly insists that the child should already sleep. Over time, your child can identify with the "baby" prop and sees that it eventually goes to sleep. The key here is to show through your skit that the parents always assure the child that they will always be there for him.

Chapter 6: How To Use Simple Steps To Help Your Kids Sleep In 48 Hours

The rule of these steps

What comes to your mind when someone mentions the Cry it out (CIO) method to you? I'm pretty sure that your maternal instincts kick in and that makes you all judgmental about the person mentioning it. Cry it out method is a practice that is highly misunderstood by most of the people out there until they take out time to sit down and read about it. No, it isn't a single technique that tells you to leave your little one to cry in his/her crib alone until he/she gets tired enough to fall back to sleep. If this is what you're against then I'm with you as it is definitely a cruel way to force a baby to sleep but again, this isn't what CIO is.

There is more than one reason why a child may be fussy when you're helping them learn to self-soothe. You should learn the difference between if the child is crying to get your attention or if he/she really is inconvenienced and in need of your assistance.

It takes time for a baby to learn a new skill: self-soothing. We as adults can get quite fussy when it comes to change. So how can you blame a baby? Just as adults get over their temporary stress with time as they adjust, so do babies. When they are put in the crib to sleep, they may cry because they are stressed about the change. This temporary stress won't damage the baby's mental health. Instead, learning how to self-soothe will develop grit and problem-solving skills in him/her.

CIO is a technique that is a part of other methods to help you train your child to fall sleep himself/herself.

1-6 months

It is crucial to set a routine for babies as early as possible. The method that really worked for Ella and Shaun was a 3-hour cycle. I started it when they were 1 weeks old. It includes three activities:

feeding, playing and sleeping. For instance, if Ella woke up at 6 am, I would feed her at 6 am, play with her for 30 minutes and put her back to sleep around 8 am. The next feed would be at 9 am, 12 pm, 3 pm, 6 pm, 9 pm and the last feeding time would be 12 pm. In the first month, you may need to feed one more time at 3 am. Once you notice the baby doesn't wake up at 3 am, you can skip it. For Ella and Shaun, I was able to stop night feeding when they were 1 month old. The routing slightly changed when both were 3-6 months. The 3-hours circle extended to 4-hours, which means that if they woke up at 6 am, their first feed would be at 6 am, 10 am, 2 pm, 6 pm and the last feeding time would be 10 pm. All the activities will be the same: feed, play and sleep. The only difference is that you should extend playing time with the baby since his/her waking hours are longer.

In the last feed, you need to skip the playtime and put your baby to sleep right after feeding and burping. If the baby wakes up in the middle of the night or wakes up too early for no reason (poop or sickness etc.), ignore him/her so that they go back to sleep. Most of the babies should get used to the routine within 48 hours.

There was a very big difference in my experiences of sleep training Ella and Shawn. When I analyzed it, other than the differences in resistance techniques of my two little masterminds, the way I reacted to their journey of settling in the new habit played a very important role. Naturally, for Ella's sleep training, I was a new mommy and that added more stress for me. I checked up on her a few times a night in the beginning, at times this would wake her up and ultimately it used to result in both of us being unrested the following day.

After I adopted the CIO method introduced by our pediatrician, I was pretty impressed with how well the technique worked on the first night. I realized that when Ella cried a couple of times through the night, most of the times she would slip back to sleep in less than 10 minutes. I would wait for 20 minutes after the sound stopped and entered her room to check her condition. From day 2, she was sleeping soundly through the night and so was I. Because of this experience, when it is much easier to train Shaun. He was also able to sleep through a night on the second night, once I start his sleep training.

The steps above to set up routine for the baby were proven very effective not just for me but for many friends with whom I shared the technique with. Sleeping through the night is extremely beneficial for the mom and the baby. Moms, you need your energy to recharge so that you can report back to mommy duties attentively the next morning and feel confident of yourself.

There are a number of external factors that contribute to the success/failure of the CIO. Room temperature is one of these factors. The temperature of the room should neither be too hot nor too cold. Light is another factor. During the morning napping, I normally closed the curtain to make sure that the baby can sleep in the darker room.

Another thing to take into account is making sure that at this stage your baby does not get used to sleeping in your arms or falling asleep when being rocked because it will create problems for you later when the baby starts to depend on it. Similarly, make sure that the baby does not sleep while being fed either.

Example for the 3-hour cycle:

6 AM	9 AM	12 PM			
Feed	Play & Sleep	Feed	Play & Sleep	Feed	Play & Sleep
3 PM	**6 PM**	**9 PM**			
Feed	Play & Sleep	Feed	Play & Sleep	Feed	Play & Sleep
12 AM		**3 AM**	**6 AM**		
Last Feed		Sleep Optional	Feed		

6-12 months

In this stage, the method will stay the same as above. Your baby should already be habituated to a routine. One of the differences is a longer wake up time (4-5 hours), so you would need to adjust the time for each circle, from 4 hours to 4.5-5 hours for example. The other major difference is that the baby starts to have mashed food, so their food intake is much more. If your baby wakes up at 6 am, the first feed could be 6 am, 10.30 am, 3 pm, and 7.30 pm. You can skip the feed at 12 am if your baby can sleep over.

Example for the 4.5-hour cycle:

6 AM   **10:30 AM**   **3 pm**

Feed   Play & Sleep   Feed   Play & Sleep   Feed   Play & Sleep

7:30 PM   **12 AM**   **6 AM**

Feed   Play & Sleep   Optional   Sleep   Feed

Toddler

Again, the principle of the method will be similar to the previous ones. The biggest challenge would be that your little one will shift to a bed from the crib, which will give him/her the freedom to walk out and come to you after you have put him/her to bed. You will find yourself to be facing a completely different ball game.

When Ella moved to the bed, she'd always jump out after we put her sleep, followed us to our room and asked us to stay with her in the room. I was completely clueless about how to deal with this new situation. It is different from the previous model: the baby was confined to the crib and you can put them down and leave. I was back to square one, staying 1 hour or more to accompany and pat her. Most of the time, she was guarded. The moment I removed my hand from her body, she would wake up and cry. The worst part is that she would wake up a couple of times in the middle of the night and run to our room. It was a big battle to put her back to sleep. None of us could have a healthy and consistent sleep, which resulted in everyone being frustrated and upset.

Luckily, we got the advice from one of our close friends, Dina, who is also a baby sleeping consultant. She explained to us what we did was actually preventing Ella from self-soothing. Because Ella was expecting we would leave, naturally, she was guarded and couldn't have sound sleep. Children's brain hasn't developed proper logic thinking, so as parents, we need to send a direct message to help them have the right behavior. We need to let her know if she doesn't sleep in the night time, no one is going to play with her. Dina asked us to reestablish the bedtime routine to make sure it suits Ella's development and told us how to act after we put her to sleep.

Here is the example that we reset Ella's sleeping schedule:

7 am   1 pm   2 pm   9 pm   9:30 pm

Wake up   Nap Time   Wake up from Nap   Start   the Bedtime Routine   Turn on night light & walk out from the room.

Important things when you reset the schedule:

•   Don't let him/her take a long nap that exceeds 2 hours as it will make it harder for your child to go to sleep at night.

•   The afternoon nap and the bedtime should be at least 7-8 hours apart.

•   For the 1st sleep training night, you can even prolong the bedtime to 10 or 10.30 pm so you can leverage your kid's fatigue. Make sure that your child has some physical activities after nap so he/she is tired.

After you reestablish the sleep schedule, you would need to build nighttime routine to let your children understand it is a bedtime.

There are several things that you can do to prepare your child's mind for bed. A repeated nighttime routine will let your child wind down and give him/her hint that it is a bedtime. Here are some tips you should consider when you set up nighttime routine:

- Start the routine 20 to 30 minutes before bedtime.
- Try to keep the activities subtle so that the kid can calm down before bedtime.
- Reading bedtime stories is highly recommended. Both of my kids always look forward to choosing the storybooks and enjoy intimacy with us before bedtime.

After tucking the baby in and kissing him/her good night, you need to leave the room immediately. The trick to stop them from coming to your room is to lock yourself in your room. Don't lock their room or confine them in their room. By doing this, you are sending a direct message to your kid: it is sleeping time, and no one will play with you.

Ignore the fuss he/she makes outside of your door. No attention from you will make them go back to their bed and sleep eventually. Most of the children will change their behavior and adopt the new routine within 48 hours.

The first day of training will be toughest for most of parents. Though Dina warned us about the duration of the cry we may experience, it was still much harder to handle it.

After I put Ella to bed on that night, I told her I won't stay in her room to pat her to sleep and she needs to stay in the bed. Ella didn't realize the game was changing until I left and stayed in my room. She started to run to our door and stayed there crying.

During the hour she was crying outside the door, Jack and I needed to hold each other's hand not to open the door. Since we were exhausted and lacking in proper sleep for months, we desperately wanted the technique to work. We were expecting Ella would even sleep outside our door, but she went to back to her bed and slept after an hour of crying.

On the 2nd night, we were expecting the same pattern to repeat but a miracle happened. When she ran to our door and saw the door was closed, she ran back to her room immediately and cried for 10 minutes before drifting to sleep. Jack and I looked at each other and couldn't believe that it actually worked on the 2nd night as what Dina mentioned.

After the 2nd night, Ella repeated the same pattern 2-3 times for the next 2 weeks, but she always went back to her bed and slept quickly.

Things to consider

To implement this, there are a few things that parents need to take into account while instilling healthy sleeping habits in toddlers. I will address them in this section.

1. The sense of safety:

Firstly, you must ensure that when you do sleep training, the child's sleeping environment stays consistent and safe. Since you will leave his/her room door open, make sure the living area is tidy for him/her to wander and also keep a small lamp or the toilet light on to prevent him/her from tripping. To be on the safe side, consider baby-proofing the apartment.

2. Offering Minimum Soothing

Knowing when to step in to soothe the child yourself is important. Generally, kids don't cry over 30-40 minutes (except 1st night). If your child is crying over that time, check on him/her and offer some water. If your kid is not ill and just fussing around to get your attention, you should give him minimum soothing and walk out.

If the child abruptly stops crying, don't walk into the room as soon as it happens because the child is often in the phase of drifting back to sleep. It is best to wait 20-30 minutes before checking up on him/her. If you go in right away, the crying and fussing around will start again.

3. Stick to the routine:

Sticking to the routine, no matter what is essential. This means, even if the previous night, your baby didn't go to sleep on time or any event happened that disrupted the routine, don't let it ruin the next day's routine. Wake the child up on time and don't extend the napping time. The child may be fussy for the day but in the long-term, this will benefit the whole family.

Questions when you adopt this approach

Q: Should I still wake the baby up at 7 am if she remained awake a lot during the night?

The answer to this is yes, you should. Letting the child sleep will make him more active and push down the napping time, which will further push down the bedtime and ultimately ruin the bedtime routine that you worked so hard to establish. Your child might be a little fussier than usual during the day but trust me, starting from the next day; everything will go back to normal.

Q: What if the baby wakes up at 4:30 am or 5 am?

If the child wakes up in the middle of the night, you must ignore him/her and let him/her go back to sleep.

Q: It's been 3-4 days, but the child is still crying. Why isn't it getting better?

If it's been 3-4 days and the process isn't working, this means that you're doing something wrong. Though it is normal, working within 48 hours for most of the cases, you should expect kids will test you on the 4th or 5th day. Eventually, he/she should be going to bed within 15-20 minutes.

The common mistake that parents make is that they put the child in a bed after they fall asleep. The key is to tuck them in when they are drowsy but not asleep. This is to ensure that the child is learning to fall asleep him/herself. Getting this step right is crucial otherwise the whole process will fail for a number of reasons. One of them is that the child is not learning to fall asleep by himself/herself. The other is that when they wake up in the middle of the night and cannot find you beside themselves, they will panic, which will result in the adrenaline rush and the traces of sleep will disappear.

The other common mistake is inappropriate sleep timings. If your baby is taking long naps or you're not waking them up on time in the morning, they won't experience fatigue at night, which will keep them up. Make sure that there are 7-8 hours between afternoon nap and bedtime.

If you did all of the above properly, the baby is still crying after day 4 and 5, you should check with your pediatrician or sleeping consultant to identify if there is some other problem.

Q: After we come back from holiday or after someone visits us, how can we get back to the sleep routine?

Kids would have some free pass while holidaying or when someone visits and stays with us. It is always very difficult to bring the kids back to the routine. The trick is that you need to be back to sleep training immediately after a holiday or any break, so they can see the difference and get back to the sleeping routine quickly.

Q: Will this method affect kids' mental development?

Kids' resilience is greater than you think. Such short-term stress is different from the long-term one. Instead of affecting their mental development, this method can help them learn how to couple with the stress and behave properly. As long as you do this with love, the kids would receive the message.

Chapter 7: Importance Of Establishing A Good Bedtime Routine

Whether you're using a self-soothing method or another no-tears technique, parents must understand the importance of developing a bedtime routine first. It helps you win half the battle if you could somehow communicate with your baby what to expect next, and you get just that by having a consistent bedtime ritual. Babies really do appreciate the consistency and predictability of a good bedtime routine. They need to feel relaxed and be in an environment that tells them it's time to sleep. It is important to find a right bedtime routine for your baby as early as you possibly can. Aim to have a pattern established by the time your baby is about 8 weeks old.

For a sleep routine to be successful, you need to ensure that it is short and simple. Once again, a 20-minute routine will suffice, and it could be as simple as first a warm bath and then diaper and jammies followed by a story in the rocking chair. However, the fact is that different babies have different sleep needs, so you have to find a combination of what seems best for your baby.

The Feeding Schedule

With newborns, it's all about calories and getting their tummies full. Newborns need a set amount of calories a day. We can eat three meals a day and get all the calories we need to sustain us throughout the night without us waking up hungry at some point during the night.

Infants, on the other hand, need to eat throughout the night because they haven't reached enough calories and need to eat more. One of the reasons they have to eat so often is because their stomachs are so tiny at this point in development. If their stomachs were larger, they wouldn't need to eat as often because they would be able eat more in one sitting like us. As your baby gets older, s/he will eat more and it will sustain them for longer periods of time.

When you first bring your baby home, you'll find that your baby probably wants to eat every two to three hours, both morning and at night. Most pediatricians will recommend that you let your baby dictate when s/he wants to eat for the first few weeks.

After the first few weeks, however, you can start to implement more of a regulated feeding schedule. If you really want your baby to sleep through the night, feed your baby more often during the day. In this manner, s/he will not need to eat as often during the night. Even if your baby isn't crying or signaling to you that they want to eat, feed them anyway.

At first, they may not eat much, but eventually they will grow accustomed to the feeding schedule and will start to eat more and more at each feeding and less during the night. Below is a feeding schedule you can try out. According to this schedule, you would be feeding your baby every 2 ½ hours starting at 7:30 AM.

The feedings will be at:

7:30 AM, 10:00 AM, 12:30 PM, 3:00 PM, 5:30 PM, 8:00 PM, 10:30 PM, and so on.

Let your baby feed for as long as s/he wants if you are breastfeeding, and if you are bottle feeding, prepare plenty of formula. You will quickly learn how much s/he will drink each time. If your baby is napping during a scheduled feeding time, wake them up. You will be grateful later during the night when they sleep longer.

Some moms even shorten the time period to 2 hours; however, some babies struggle to eat that frequently. You can try both to determine what works best for you and your baby.

Feeding schedules are rigorous, and you will feel like you are feeding your baby constantly at first. And realistically, it doesn't leave you with much time to get other things done. For instance, if you need to go to the grocery store, you'll feed your baby and have to run quickly in order to make it back in time for their next feeding time. Eventually, as your baby grows older, you can stretch the times to three hours but only as their stomach grows bigger and they can handle more milk or formula.

By giving them as much milk or formula as they can eat throughout the day, you increase the likelihood of them staying asleep longer during the night without needing to eat. At first, they will probably still need at least one or two feedings during the night because their stomach is still so small, but compare that to waking every two or three hours to eat. You will get stretches of four hours or more after just a few days of implementing a strong feeding schedule.

Help Your Baby Get Rid of Pent-Up Energy

After some time has passed since they were fed and burped, your baby will sleep better at night if you help them get rid of any pent-up energy in their system. Different activities will help you achieve this task. You can help them dance a bit to the tune of a catchy song, let them bounce in their bouncer, or even give your little one a "horsey" ride. These types of activities will leave your baby feeling more relaxed before bedtime if they are followed by calmer and quieter activities such as giving them a bath or reading them a storybook.

Give Your Baby a Warm Bath

A bath will go a long way in making your baby feel relaxed, especially after a few hours of play. Let your baby sit in warm water for a soothing experience. Recent research conducted in the UK reveals that almost 60% of babies have a bath every night, with all of them spending an average of 15 minutes in the water. However, if you happen to notice signs indicating that your baby is irritated or even too excited during baths, you may be better off leaving this activity out of your bedtime ritual.

Wash Your Baby's Hands and Face

When a bath is out of the question, you can include washing in your routine. Start by washing your baby's face and hands. Afterwards, brush their teeth a bit — the earlier they get used to that, the better. Lastly, a diaper change may also give your baby a signal that it's time to sleep.

Give Your Baby Verbal Reassurance

You can simply have a quick chat with your little man or girl before you put them in their crib for sound, restful sleep. Talking to your baby will be a relaxing experience not only for your baby but for you as well.

Read a Bedtime Story

Get a storybook with colorful pictures. You can lay your baby in their crib and gently rock it from side to side while you read for a few minutes. It is a good idea to start this routine when your baby is as young as 8 weeks.

Say Goodnight to Their Favorite Toys

Walk around with your baby in your arms and say goodnight to his or her favorite toys or objects. It's an interesting activity to include in the bedtime routine, and many parents have found it quite effective because babies enjoy being carried.

Chapter 8: Sleep Solutions and Strategies

It is important to understand that no two babies are going to be the exact same. Even if the babies are siblings, they are likely going to have different sleep needs. What works to get one baby to sleep soundly will not work for another. There is some trial and error involved as you figure out what solutions and strategies work best for you and your baby. Do not be dismayed if your sister or best friend tells you this method worked like a dream for her, but your baby absolutely refuses to cooperate. Everybody has different ways of doing things and it is just going to take a little practice to figure out what your sleeping trick is going to be.

Please know that you cannot give up on a single solution after one night. Give it a week or so to give your child the chance to adapt to your new method. If it still isn't working, then it is probably a good time to tweak your habits or try something new altogether.

Preventing SIDS

Sleeping is important to a baby's health, but proper sleeping positions are crucial in the prevention against SIDs. Medical professionals recommend infants be put to sleep on their backs. Your parents or older babysitter will tell you this is wrong, but things have changed over the past 20 years. It has been revealed that the back is best when it comes to laying a baby in bed.

All those stuffed toys are cute and cuddly, but they should never be placed in the baby's crib, cradle or bassinet. Along with that, you don't want your baby's bed to be too soft. The mattress needs to be firm. Don't put too many blankets on your baby at night. Warm clothing and a single blanket are usually enough. When possible, sleep in the same room with your baby those first weeks and months. You will be in tune to your baby's breathing and will likely hear when he is in distress.

Lastly, don't smoke around your baby—ever. If at all possible, keep your baby away from all secondhand smoke. Some experts believe putting a baby to sleep with a pacifier is also helpful in preventing SIDs, but the correlation between the two hasn't been confirmed. Giving your baby a pacifier when he goes to bed can help the baby sleep better during the first 12 months.

Birth to 4 Months

It seems like you have waited forever to get that little bundle of joy in your arms, but now you are hoping to put the baby down for a little while so you can get some sleep. The first few months after the baby is born are an exciting time. You will likely have lots of visitors who want to see and hold the baby. All the activity can make it difficult for you and your baby to settle into a nice routine. It is tough to plan visits around a newborn's schedule. They need a lot of sleep and a constant stream of visitors can be difficult to manage.

The following sleep solutions can help you get your baby to sleep after a busy day of visiting:

Stop playing - Your newborn will only be awake for short periods of time before he starts to get sleepy. He may want to stay awake a bit longer so he can absorb his surroundings and most importantly, study you. When you notice your baby getting sleepy or it is time for a nap or bed, it is time to stop playing. Don't make direct eye contact with the little one as you rock him to sleep or feed him. Eye contact is stimulating to the baby and he will be eager to stay awake all night watching you.

Put baby down - When the baby has been awake for an hour or so or you can tell he is getting sleepy, put the baby in his bed and stay nearby. It is an excellent opportunity to teach the baby how to fall asleep on his own. It helps to have some white noise to help soothe the baby. It may be the radio, television or even the dishwasher running. When it is too quiet, the baby may struggle to fall asleep.

Infant swings - The gentle swaying of a swing is soothing to some babies—not all. Recline the seat, strap the baby in and put the swing on the low setting to gently rock the baby to sleep. This gives you a free moment as well as puts baby to sleep. You can try moving the baby to his bed after he has been lulled to sleep in the swing. This takes some practice and you will have to learn whether or not your child appreciates the move after he has fallen asleep.

Crying it out - This is something that has lost a lot of favor with parents of today's generation. Infants cry for a particular reason, not because they want to. A whimper or a little fussing is considered okay to leave alone to let the child try and soothe himself back to sleep. However, a constant cry usually indicates the child is distressed and needs attention. When the baby fusses, stand near the bed and quietly talk to the baby to try and allay any troubles. Sometimes a comforting hand on the baby's abdomen is all that is needed to give the baby a little comfort knowing mom or dad is nearby.

Turn out the lights - Use room darkening shades, blinds or curtains to help block the light when it is naptime or when you want the baby to sleep past sunrise. You want to help train the child that darkness is associated with sleep. By setting the mood in the room, your baby will soon start picking up on the signal that it is time to slow down and sleep. A nightlight is perfectly fine and advisable. Be aware also of intrusions such as street lights and your neighbors motion activated garage lights that can split the darkness in your baby's room.

Old fashioned rocking - Rocking chairs have been used to rock babies to sleep for hundreds of years for a reason—they work! A nice slow rocking motion is very soothing. Let the baby snuggle close and he will likely fall asleep in no time. There are a couple of different approaches to putting the baby down. You will need to figure out what works best for your baby.

1-When the baby is quiet and content and on the verge of sleep, gently put him in bed.

Allow the baby to fall into a deep sleep on his own.

2-Wait until the baby is in a deep sleep before placing him on his back in bed.

Swaddling - Newborns have been living in a cramped area with their limbs wrapped tightly about them for months. When they are introduced to the bright, loud world, it is only natural they would feel safer when wrapped up tight. Swaddling gives them that safety and comfort they need in order to relax enough to let sleep take them. The nurses in the hospital will typically show parents how to properly swaddle a baby. There are also plenty of blankets with Velcro that make it easy to swaddle the child. Before putting the baby to bed, swaddle the child.

4 Months to 1 Year

By this age, your baby is learning more about sleep habits and will be more prepared to accept routines. This is an excellent time for you to start establishing bedtime routines and established bedtimes.

Soothing bath - A soothing, warm bath is one way to signal to the baby that bedtime is imminent. The warm water helps relax the baby. You can use some lavender infused baby washes to take advantage of the calming effects of lavender. Keep play time to a minimum as you start setting the mood for sleep.

Rituals - Establish a ritual that suits your baby and you. If it is the warm bath, a fresh diaper, nursing/bottle and rocking for five minutes before laying the child in bed, go for it. Be consistent to teach the child what each of the steps indicates. When it is bath time, your baby will learn bedtime is imminent. He will start to settle and look forward to the feeding and cuddling before bed. Your ritual may be different. Do what works best for you!

Give a full belly - Babies of this age will not need to eat as often as newborns, but they will still need to eat every few hours. You can help your baby sleep longer by starting to fill the tummy an hour or two before bed. Instead of feeding every three hours, feed the baby two hours before bed and then again just before bedtime. This will hopefully earn you a longer block of sleep before the child is hungry again.

Slings or Mobys - About 30 minutes before it is time for the child to go down for a nap or bed, put the baby in a sling or Moby and go about your business. The gentle swaying of your movement, combined with the closeness and sound of your heart beating will help lull the child into sleep. It is also the signal to the child that it is no longer time to play.

Pacing - Walking around the living room with the baby snuggled up against your shoulder is an old trick. The movement is soothing to the baby. Singing or talking often helps soothe the child. The vibration in your chest as you talk to the baby or to others is comforting. Throw the baby's favorite blanket over him and rub the back while walking around the room. As the baby gets older, this can prove more difficult as the child gets heavier.

Gadgets - You have seen the plethora of Teddy Bears that "breathe," mobiles, crib toys and other gear that is all designed to create white noise to remind the child of being in the womb. It is supposed to be soothing and help lull the child into a deep sleep. The truth is these things only work with some babies. Some children are agitated by the constant noise. However, they do work and your baby just may be one of those who can fall asleep to the sounds produced by these gadgets. One recommendation—if it a singing, humming or talking gizmo, find one that allows you to record your voice for the child to fall asleep too just in case the toy is not always around.

1 year to 2 years

By a year of age, your child will be familiar with your bedtime habits. If you have a ritual in place, keep with it if it is working. It will likely need tweaking to accommodate your child's development. If you are still struggling to get your child to sleep and to stay asleep, try some of these techniques. It is never too late to implement a new ritual that is more effective.

Loosen up - Newborns appreciate swaddling, while babies and toddlers prefer to have room to move. Keep the blankets to a minimum. A single cotton blanket will likely be enough. You will know what works best for your baby. Some babies will want a couple of blankets to feel the heaviness, while others will want room to move freely. If you are worried the child will kick off the blankets and be cold at night, put the baby in a footed sleeper.

Quiet the room - At this age, noises will affect a child's ability to sleep. They tend to be stimulating to the more active and alert child. While typical household noise is usually fine, do what you can to limit sudden, loud sounds. Disconnect the doorbell so nobody will ring it, oil the hinges on squeaky doors, put the dog outside if it tends to bark and turn your cell phone to vibrate. Every child is different! Your child may sleep better with some background music or water running. If you discover your child is struggling to stay asleep or fall asleep, try playing some very low background noise.

Winding down - Toddlers are very active and can automatically switch gears when they are told it is bedtime. You need to start the bedtime ritual well in advance. Give the child at least an hour to start transitioning from playtime to sleep time. It could be something like this, dinner, bath, story time and then bed.

Cry it out - This does not mean the child is left in his bed to cry for hours on end. The child is learning coping mechanisms at this age. If you put the child to bed after the standard ritual and he still struggles a bit to wind down, leave him be. Let the child lie in his bed for a bit. The child may cry a little, call for you or even talk to himself. Stay out of the room and let the child try and work through it alone. This can be a little difficult at first. The first time you do this, it may take 15 minutes, the second and third nights it may take 10 minutes. If you see progress, you will know it is working. If it is difficult to hear your child cry, try to keep yourself busy. Wash the dishes, fold the laundry or try and watch television to keep your mind off the crying baby.

Cool and comfortable - We all sleep a little better when the room is slightly cool. There is a line between cool and comfortable and too cold. Turn down the thermostat a couple of degrees so the child doesn't get too warm and end up waking up. You will find you sleep better in a cooler environment as well.

2 years to 5 years

By now, your toddler is capable of going to sleep and sleeping through the night. Capable does not always mean it happens. You will need to create an ideal sleeping environment, including a ritual that gets your child ready to sleep for at least 10 hours. You will want to make sure the child has used the restroom, gotten a last drink of water and is prepared to sleep without interruption. Sometimes, it isn't the getting to bed that is the problem with children of this age. It is the staying in bed that interrupts the child's sleep and yours.

Comfort - Make your child's room and bed as cozy as possible. You want to create the perfect environment for sleeping. Special sheets and blankets are one way you can make it more inviting. A big kid bed (toddler bed) with rails is often enough encouragement for the child to go to bed alone. Tuck in the child, turn on a night light and leave the room. Make sure the room is dark and quiet. Room darkening shades are very helpful during the summer when early bedtimes mean it is still daylight outside.

Story time - Your toddler will have the ability to get up out of bed as often he pleases. You can help encourage the child to stay in bed by spending 5 to 10 minutes in the room with the child while he lies in bed. Read a story, talk about the day for a few minutes or sing lullabies while the child lies down. This will make the child feel more comfortable about the pending separation. The child needs to feel safe in his bed and with you spending a little time helping him make the transition, he will.

Avoiding nightmares/bad dreams - Toddlers are beginning to develop an active imagination at this stage. Your child may get out of bed and come running for you if he has bad dreams. If it happens regularly, your sleep schedule can be thrown off. Monitor television programs that could be causing the dreams. Bedtime stories should be free of monsters, dragons or other fictional creatures that are making their way into your child's dreams. If a bad dream does awaken the child, soothe the child and let him know it is okay. Avoid telling the child it isn't real, because in their minds it is very real. Don't spend 30 minutes explaining bad dreams. Lie with the child a few minutes and reassure him before leaving the room.

Reassurance - If your child is new to a toddler bed, he may feel a little insecure. If the child calls out for you every time you leave the room or gets out of bed and follows you, you will need to reassure him everything is okay. Insist the child stays in bed. Check on the child every 5 minutes or so. He will see you are still there and will feel better. The next day, you can check in every 8 minutes and slowly make the time intervals longer. This helps assure the child you are nearby if he needs you.

Keeping the child in bed - There are plenty of creative excuses for getting out of bed. The need to use the potty, the need for a drink or whatever excuses the child can come up with. When this happens, turn the child around and put him back in bed. Tuck him in without getting into a discussion. You may need to do this repeatedly the first night, but it will gradually decrease as the child learns you will not be swayed. Do not get angry and shout at the child. Stay calm and simply put him back in bed.

Chapter 9: More Health Tips for Mother and Child

This chapter essentially contains three sections, namely, a section on postpartum health, one of the more important yet neglected aspects of motherhood; a section on how to choose the right pediatrician for your baby, which is crucial in determining the health of your little one throughout his formative years; and a section on other related health issues that you should consider.

Postpartum Health Management

One of the most common misconceptions about childbirth is that only the newborn baby requires adequate care and support upon birth. However, it is also important to take care of the mother who has just given birth, because she is also just as vulnerable to risks and even possible complications after giving birth. This is especially true if the mother does not seek nor undergo proper postpartum healthcare. In this section, we provide information regarding postpartum health, including an overview of what the postpartum period is, how postpartum healthcare should be managed, and the goals a new mother and her doctor should set for herself six weeks after giving birth. Armed with such information, mothers should be able to manage their health and well----being which, in turn, will allow them to fully take care of their newborn baby.

The Postpartum Period

A lot of people believe that the pregnancy timeline ends once a baby is born. However, as a new mother, you should continue to closely monitor your health, with support from healthcare professionals, to ensure that your postpartum health is being properly evaluated and managed.

The postpartum period begins immediately after delivery and lasts up to eight weeks after childbirth. During this crucial period, you may experience discomfort, uneasiness and even complications, which should immediately be reported to your doctor. In fact, it is highly recommended that you have your postpartum appointment with your doctor at about 6 or 8 weeks after giving birth to your baby.

Obviously, the postpartum period is an important part of the pregnancy timeline, because this is the time at which you (your mind and your body) are adjusting to changes after delivery and to your changing roles as a new mother as well. How you cope with motherhood largely depends on whether or not you will be able to meet your postpartum health goals (more on this will be discussed later). For now, let us take a look at the basic objectives of a successful postpartum period transition. During the postpartum period, the following goals should be met:

- Proper management of the mother's physical, psychological, and emotional health;
- Fostering of healthy and supportive interactions among the mother, her partner, and their baby;
- Provision of sufficient knowledge that shall allow the mother to properly take care of her newborn baby; and
- Development and improvement of the mother's parenting skills.

During the postpartum period, the physiological changes you will experience include fluctuating blood pressure, excessive blood discharge, shifting of your internal organs to their normal positions, increased demand for rest, and so on. As for the psychological and emotional changes, you may experience increased feelings of exhaustion, depression, guilt, inability to cope, and so on.

If left unchecked, these changes can develop into possible complications that will ultimately harm your overall health. Thus, it is important to pay close attention to your health during the postpartum period.

Things to Expect After Giving Birth

As mentioned earlier, your body goes through tremendous changes after giving birth, and part of successful postpartum healthcare is to ensure that you are able to handle these changes and manage them safely with the help of your doctor and your family. Just as your body experiences drastic changes while being pregnant with your baby, drastic changes after giving birth can also be expected. This is because your body is attempting to get back to its normal shape and condition before it changed to accommodate a baby inside. This subsection provides a list of what you should expect after giving birth.

Vaginal discharge

Immediately after delivery and many weeks after that, you will experience varying degrees of vaginal discharge or what is called lochia. While your baby is still inside your womb, he is enveloped by layers of tissue and blood that lined the uterus. When your baby comes out, this lining will be shed, like menstruation. However, lochia is different in that you will expel large amounts of lochia that range in color from bright red to yellow or white. The bleeding is heavier and has a bright red color for the first three or four days after delivery, then turns pink, then dark red/brown, and finally white or yellow as the weeks pass. Lochia is shed gradually but can be discharged in clots when making sudden movements. It can even turn bright red again with excessive activities.

Cramping

Cramping, which is also called "afterpain," is common among women who just gave birth. When you experience cramping, this means that your uterus is contracting back to its normal size. Severe cramping can be experienced especially after two or three days of delivery and eventually lessens in about a week. It is said that afterpains are usually worse for seconds or third----time mothers because their uterus requires much more effort to get back to its old size, compared with first----time mothers who still have muscle tone in their uterus. In addition, breastfeeding moms also report cramping. This is because the baby's sucking initiates the release of the hormone called oxytocin, which then triggers contractions in the uterus that lead to cramping.

Swelling

Also called "edema," swelling is a common accompaniment of pregnancy. However, swelling can also occur after a mother gives birth. Swelling after childbirth is often due to the body's retention of excessive fluids a few weeks before you gave birth. Thus, during the postpartum period, you will still experience swelling, usually 2 days to a week after delivery. Should swelling persist after a week, or if swelling is accompanied by severe headache and pain in the extremities, then you should call your doctor's attention for possible high blood pressure. Meanwhile, if only one leg continues to swell, with excessive pain, you may have what is called "deep vein thrombosis." In this case, immediate medical attention is also required.

Problems in urination

In relation to your body's need to expel all remaining fluids that have been retained during pregnancy, you may experience excessive urination or even temporary urinary incontinence. This is because your kidney is working double time to remove excess liquid from your system and restore it to its pre----pregnancy state. For those who have had an episiotomy, urinating for the first few days after delivery can be terribly painful. Nevertheless, the pain will also go away after some time. In addition, due to the damaged ligaments and muscles in your crotch area, you may also find it difficult to urinate. However, this reflex will be back to normal in as early as one week. For faster recovery, Kegel exercises are recommended so that the mother can regain control of her muscles in that region of her body.

Perspiration

Similar to excessive urination described above, your body also gets rid of excessive fluids through your sweat glands. Hence, perspiration is also a common experience a few days after giving birth.

Constipation

This is one of the most inconvenient experiences any new mother has after delivery. Postpartum constipation is due to several reasons. First, the abdominal muscles that have been severely stretched during pregnancy have yet to function normally a few days after delivery. Second, your intestines may not yet be able to operate in the same way that they have before you got pregnant. Since this can be quite painful especially for a mother who has had episiotomy, it is suggested that you use a stool softener. At the same time, you can also follow a strict diet consisting of fresh fruits and vegetables, lots of water, and foods that are rich in fiber. At the same time, Kegel exercises can also be done to gain full control of the muscles associated with bowel movement.

Soreness

The sensitive area between the rectum and the vagina is called the "perineum," which usually becomes sore and extremely painful, especially because it is stretched and torn and then stitched up during normal delivery. To relieve soreness, ice packs are usually placed over the area about 12 to 24 hours after once the perineum is stitched up. To eliminate possible infections, the area should be kept clean and dry. Once the stitches are dissolved, soreness lessens for a period of about 1 to 2 weeks after giving birth.

Postpartum Healthcare Goals

According to the Association of Reproductive Health Professionals, proper postpartum healthcare management requires that you and your doctor set goals that not only monitor your progress six weeks after giving birth but also facilitates quicker and safer transition back to your pre----pregnancy state. The so----called Six----Week Postpartum Health Goals include the following: Weight Loss, Balanced Nutrition, Physical Examination, and Provision of Information on Sexuality, Contraception, and Emotional Adjustment.

Weight loss

The goal of losing weight has got to be the most common among all mothers who have just given birth. Women pack on a lot of pounds during pregnancy so it requires a lot of work. Fortunately, this is a manageable goal with proper diet and exercise. However, before starting on an exercise routine, get clearance from your doctor first.

Nutrition

To facilitate safe weight loss of about 5 lbs per month, also consider consuming around 1,800 calories a day, mainly though foods rich in iron and protein (lean beef, seafood), low----fat dairy products, and green, leafy vegetables. Taking nutritional supplements, especially those that augment your iron and calcium intake, is also recommended.

Physical examination

After birth, you must be raring to get back to your normal routines. However, you need to have your regular physical examinations to ensure that your body is in top condition and to avoid possible complications. During your physical examination, you may ask your doctor about related concerns you may have regarding your vaginal discharge, soreness from breastfeeding, problems with bowel movement and constipation, appearance of varicose veins, proper healing of your perineum (for those who had natural childbirth) or abdominal wound (for those who had a C----section).

Information on sexuality and contraception

One of the goals of postpartum healthcare management is to you ease back into your pre----pregnancy routines, one of which is resuming sexual activities with your partner. Sexual desires soon come back a few weeks after giving birth. For those who opt not to breastfeed their baby, ovulation may occur in as early as 45 days after giving birth. Thus, it is important to explore this aspect of postpartum healthcare with your doctor. For example, when exactly will you be fertile again? Are you considering family planning options? When can you safely have sex with your partner again? How can you reduce discomfort when having sex? These are important concerns so do not be embarrassed to ask your doctor about them.

Emotional adjustment

Aside from dealing with physiological changes in your body, you also have to deal with your emotional and mental condition after giving birth. Many mothers with newborn babies have to rest and recuperate for some time at home. This seclusion, along with the added tasks of taking care of a baby round----the----clock may result in feelings of isolation, severe exhaustion, crankiness, moodiness, nervousness, loss, and so on. In severe cases, such feelings may lead to postpartum depression, thus, it is important that you express your concerns with your doctor. Some of the things you can do to minimize these "baby blues" are as follows:

- Touch base with families and friends;
- Set some "me time" within the day (like taking a long, luxurious bath while your baby is sleeping);
- Join forums for newborn moms; and
- Go on brisk walks outside (with or without your baby) if weather conditions are good.

Possible Complications

The common symptoms experienced by women after giving birth have been discussed above. To recap, these may include vaginal discharge, pain and soreness in the perineum, difficulty in bowel movement and urination, as well as swelling, to name a few. While these are expected, you should also watch out for complications that may arise when these are left unaddressed. Generally, the following indicators serve as red flags that you should see your doctor immediately:

- Extreme pain and swelling in your lower extremities
- Persistent pain in the perineum
- Excessive bleeding or discharge
- Sore and overly swollen breasts
- Burning sensation while urinating
- Vomiting
- Headache and nausea
- Feelings of depression and lack of interest in taking care of your baby

Let us now take a look at some possible complications you may have during the postpartum period

Uterine infection

After giving birth, the placenta is supposed to be discharged naturally about 20 minutes after delivery. If some parts are not expelled and remain in the uterus, this can lead to uterine infection. Symptoms of infection include discharge with a very foul odor, extremely high WBC count, very high fever, rapid heart rate, and swollen uterus. If left untreated, this could lead to toxic shock, and possibly, death.

Hemorrhage

Though it occurs in very few cases of delivery, hemorrhage is the third common cause of maternal death. Hemorrhage may arise in cases of multiple births, lengthy labor period, and uterine infection. This complication can also be due to damage/tears in the cervix and uterus as well as the failure of the uterus to contract (and expel the placenta) following delivery. Doctors can immediately treat hemorrhage should it occur at the hospital, but upon discharge, the mother should immediately report if hemorrhage occurs at home.

Infection of the kidney

A kidney infection may occur when the bladder becomes infected and spreads bacteria to the kidney. Accompanying symptoms of kidney infection include frequent urination, burning sensation while peeing, lower back pain, and very high fever. Again, the mother should report these symptoms to her doctor so that antibiotics (oral or IV) can be immediately prescribed.

Infection from a C----section

This kind of infection usually occurs when the mother fails to follow instructions regarding proper care of a C----section incision. You may be infected if you observe the following symptoms: the wound fails to heal after the prescribed period, presence of pus, the surrounding skin is swollen, and so on.

Mastitis

Mastitis or breast infection can also arise during the postpartum period. This is usually indicated by swelling, tenderness, and reddened patches on the breast. As with other kinds of infection, you may experience very high fever, nausea, vomiting, and chills. Your doctor will simply prescribe antibiotics as a form of treatment. Although mastitis does not affect the quality of your breast milk, do check with your doctor if you can continue breastfeeding your baby while under medication.

Postpartum depression

Postpartum depression is one of the most cited psychological complications that may occur after giving birth. It affects 10% to 20% of mothers who have recently given birth and is accompanied by symptoms such as anxiety, despair, lack of energy, fear, lack of interest in one's baby, hallucinations, and even the desire to harm those around. Postpartum depression is often attributed to the combined effects of physical trauma due to childbirth, exhaustion/lack of sleep, and changing hormonal levels after giving birth.

While it is normal to experience "baby blues," such feeling can progress to postpartum depression or even postpartum psychosis if left untreated. If you observe the following symptoms, then it is important to speak with your doctor right away:

- No energy or drive to do anything;
- Insomnia;
- Migraines and heart palpitations
- Overeating
- Restlessness and irritability
- Constantly depressed and sad
- Problems in making decisions or being extremely worried about the baby
- Not having any interest in the baby
- Having thoughts of harming oneself or the baby

Certainly, the easiest way to get rid of postpartum depression is by actively taking steps to avoid having feelings such as those listed above. You can ask your family and friends to help you with this as well as seek professional guidance from your doctor.

Remember that postpartum depression can only be treated properly once you report it to the doctor. Thus, do not be embarrassed about having these feelings. Be open and seek help so that you can live a healthier life after giving birth and take proper care of your baby.

How to Choose the Right Doctor for Your Baby

The previous subsection discussed postpartum healthcare management, which provides various information and ways, by which a mother can take care of herself after giving birth. In this second subsection of the chapter, we will introduce another related aspect of motherhood, which is finding the right pediatrician for your baby.

It is very important to find the right doctor for your baby for several reasons. First, you will be making well----baby visits to the doctor's clinic on a regular basis for the first year of your baby's life and even beyond that. Second, your baby's doctor will be the prime source of information for anything related to your baby's health. Third, your baby's pediatrician will be partly responsible for the decisions you will make regarding your baby. For these reasons, you have to be careful in making this decision. In the following, let us take a look at some useful tips in choosing the right doctor for your baby

Tip #1 – Identify Your Preferences

Identifying the right doctor for your baby may seem like an overwhelming and daunting task, especially for first----time parents. As mentioned above, it is an important decision that is hinged upon several factors. Among these, your preferences should play a great role in such a choice. First of all, you will be personally communicating with the doctor and will be dealing with him/her for the next year or so of your baby's life.

On the one hand, some parents would want a doctor whose expertise is on taking care of babies and young children; hence, a pediatrician would be the right choice. This choice is advantageous because a pediatrician can adeptly handle medical issues related to infants and babies. On the other hand, some parents prefer a family doctor or GP who can treat the whole family from birth. This choice is beneficial as it ensures continuity of care and consistency in reading a baby's medical issues.

In choosing a doctor for your baby, other preference points can include the following:

- Whether the doctor is easy to talk to and is approachable
- Whether the doctor interacts well with babies and young kids
- Whether the doctor is updated in the latest trends in medical treatment
- Whether the doctor invites questions from the parents
- Whether the doctor is careful in explaining medical issues in layman's terms
- Whether the clinic is comfortable, accessible, and employs helpful staff
- Whether the doctor is available even after clinic hours

Your ultimate choice may also depend on whether you have the same parenting style as the doctor or whether he or she is highly recommended by friends and families. These points shall be discussed in the following subsections.

Tip #2 – Seek Referrals From Friends And Family Members

In choosing the right doctor for your baby, the most logical approach in coming up with a list of candidates is to seek referrals from friends and families. There are no other people you would entrust with your very own life except your family members and close friends. Thus, it is only right that you seek their help when it comes to making this important decision for your baby.

Do not underestimate the power of your very own network in finding the right doctor. In this case, family member and friends can provide a wealth of information not just for possible candidates, but a whole range of suggestions and tips to help you narrow down your list of candidates. Another benefit of seeking referrals from them is having the knowledge that they have actually benefited from the services of the doctors they are recommending. Thus, you can learn valuable lessons from their actual experiences.

Aside from family and friends, however, you can also ask other trusted people in your network, such as your OB, co----workers, and even your neighbors. Just remember to take the good suggestions and integrate them into your working list based on the preference points discussed in Tip#1.

Other considerations to help you come up with a list of candidates are as follows:

- Whether the doctor is provided by your insurance network
- Whether the doctor has been certified by the American Academy of Pediatrics
- (AAP), which provides a list of certified doctors in its website

Tip #3 – Set Up An Appointment

Once you have come up with a short list of candidates, the next step is to talk to the doctors personally by setting appointments with each of them is possible. Being able to talk to the doctors face to face can help you come up with better decision since there are some things you can determine, while speaking to them face to face rather than just checking out their credentials in their websites on home pages. By paying the doctor a visit, you will be able to gauge the doctor's personality, the way he/she interacts with his little patients and their parents, the way he provides quality service and so on.

To be able to set up an appointment, you can either ask for their numbers through the referral or by checking out their websites, and then setting up an appointment by phone or by email. Whether the personnel who receives your queries and requests is polite and helpful and whether the process is a difficult or easy one, can also determine your decision. A staff member who is rude and inefficient can only give you a hard time setting up future appointments with the doctors with whom they are working.

Once you have successfully booked an appointment, you can then draw up your list of questions. Do not, however, ask these as if you are interviewing the doctor. Ask your prepared questions discreetly but directly. Some of the possible questions to ask are as follows:

- Are you available for consultation beyond clinic hours?
- Can you patiently and comprehensively explain medical issues to parents?
- Are you willing to work with the parents in coming up with a specific well----baby program for each baby?

Once you have met the candidate doctors in your list, you can now make a decision based on the information you have gathered and also on your general assessment of the doctors with whom you have set up an appointment. In making an overall assessment, perhaps it's also a good idea to choose the doctor with whom you feel a connection. This is what the final tip is about.

Tip #4 – Check For Compatibility

You and your chosen doctor shall become partners in ensuring that proper healthcare is given to your baby. This doctor should not only be adept at providing such service, but also somebody with whom you have a connection. Sometimes, the interaction between parents and their child's doctor exceeds beyond professional boundaries. As with any partnership, it is important that the doctor you will eventually choose is someone who you see as an excellent working partner for the first few years of your child's life.

Do You Have The Same Views on Parenting in General?

Working with a doctor, someone to whom you will entrust your child's health, involves making crucial decisions at several periods of your child's development stage. In this case, it is important that the doctor you will choose shares the same views you have about several things related to child rearing.

For example, does the doctor encourage breastfeeding? Is he for or against co----sleeping? If he is against co----sleeping, is he in favor of the "crying it out method?" Does he have a preference for natural or synthetic medicines? What are his views regarding vaccination? What about weaning? What are his thoughts on circumcision? Identifying answers to these questions will help you gauge whether you share the same parenting principles as your candidate doctor.

In summary, this chapter deals with the two most important players involved in your baby's delivery—you and your baby. In the first part of the chapter, the book discusses postpartum healthcare management and the related information, such as an overview of the postpartum period, the postpartum healthcare goals, and the possible complications that may arise. Meanwhile, the second part of the chapter presents useful tips of how to choose the right doctor for your baby. Mainly, you should choose a doctor who has been referred by families and friends, someone whose practice agrees well with your parenting principles, and whose personality complements yours. By taking care of yourself and your baby, both of you shall continue to live healthy lives together.

Chapter 10: Analyze

Now that you've done all you can to ensure your baby's success, he or she should have a great night of healthy sleep, right?

We wish! As any parent will tell you, even after all precautions have been taken, a baby might still have trouble sleeping. Many people feel that the reasons a baby doesn't sleep are inexplicable, just part of 'being a baby,' and not something they can do anything about.

Thankfully, that isn't the case. When babies don't sleep well, there is always an underlying cause. Using your analytical skills, you can learn to identify the underlying causes of your baby's sleepless nights, and once you have an understanding of why your baby doesn't sleep, you can start to problem-solve how to help get them on track. This is a step that you will be taking throughout your baby's development into a healthy child.

Let's go over some common obstacles that might be interfering with your baby's sleep and learn how to overcome them.

Overtiredness

If your baby is overtired, they are unlikely to sleep well at night. Even in the best of circumstances, there will be days when your baby's routine is disrupted and they miss some of that important napping time. If this happens, be prepared to take steps to help your baby fall asleep and stay asleep once evening hits.

Try this: If possible, give your baby a short make-up nap at an appropriate point in the day. If it's too late and overtiredness can't be avoided, take extra care to help your baby relax before bed, by turning down the lights, engaging in soothing routines, or giving them a gentle bath. Try to keep their environment quiet by turning off the TV and radio. You may need to hold or rock your baby to sleep to give them an extra boost, but be wary of making this a habit.

Distraction

Outside distractions can be another obstacle to healthy baby sleep. Sounds, lights, toys, and visual stimuli can all keep your baby from dropping off into slumber. Older babies and toddlers are more easily distracted by their surroundings, but babies of any age will benefit from a distraction-free environment.

Try this: Make sure that your baby's sleeping place is located in a place that can be cut off from unnecessary noise and light, such as that from a TV. Remove toys from in and around the crib or bed. If you use a nightlight, make sure that the room remains dark enough for sleepy eyes to let go of the visual stimulus all around them.

Overstimulation

Overstimulation can be another culprit blocking your baby's way to sleep. Overstimulation can come in many forms, sometimes even from your own attempts to soothe!

Try this: Avoid rowdy play or getting your baby 'wound-up' before bed. Create a calming night ritual and stick to it. Allow your baby to put himself back to sleep whenever possible; babies, just like adults, toss and turn and wake up briefly throughout the night. They don't always need your help to get back to sleep.

Hunger or Thirst

Crying is how your baby gets her needs met. Baby tummies are small. The younger your baby is, the more often that they will wake up in the night due to hunger or thirst.

Try this: If your baby is crying, check to see if they are hungry or thirsty. Often addressing these needs is all it takes to get them back to sleep. If your baby is still waking up hungry after 4-6 months, try adjusting their feeding schedule to make sure that they're getting enough to eat and drink. If the problem persists, bring it to the attention of your pediatrician.

Nightmares

Nightmares are dreams with disturbing content or emotions. If you've ever had one, you know just how frightening they can be! It's uncertain as to exactly when babies begin having nightmares, but it's thought that nightmares start to show up by your baby's first birthday. Since most dreaming happens during the second half of the night, this is when nightmares are most likely to occur.

No one is completely certain why nightmares happen, however they are usually linked to stress, illness, physical or mental/emotional discomfort, or pain. If your baby is ill, for example, you may find that they experience more nightmares. The same is true if they have a stressful day or experience separation anxiety in the hours leading up to bed time. If your baby wakes up from a nightmare, they may be distressed and have a difficult time falling back to sleep.

Try this: To calm your baby down after a nightmare, start by reassuring them of your presence. Speak in a soothing tone of voice and provide physical contact in the form of hugs or back rubs. Engage in familiar sleep routines such as rocking or walking. Stay in the room with them while they fall back to sleep.

Night terrors

Night terrors are more common in older children but may occur in toddlers as well. Babies may exhibit behavior resembling a night terror, however these may be classified as confusional arousals. To an observant parent, night terrors may appear to be like intense or extreme nightmares. When a baby or toddler experiences a night terror, they may sit up suddenly and start screaming, crying or shouting. They will appear to be experiencing intense fear and may be sweating or panting. Night terrors may last a few seconds or several minutes. The baby may or may not wake up after the night terror, and in either case will probably not remember that it has occurred. Because babies and toddlers are not aware that a night terror has happened, these are often more distressing for parents than for the baby himself.

Try this: If your baby or toddler experiences a night terror, don't try to wake them. The best thing that you can do is simply wait for the night terror to pass and watch out for any danger. Your baby probably won't realize you are there even if you do try to help. If your baby or toddler experiences night terrors, take some precautions to keep them safe, similar to those you would for sleepwalking.

Sleepwalking

Although sleepwalking usually occurs in children, your toddler has the potential to begin walking in her sleep as soon as she's learned how to do it while awake. If your toddler is sleepwalking, she may appear to be awake, or even speak to you, when in reality she is asleep and unaware of what is going on. Sleepwalking in and of itself need not reflect a disorder, however sleepwalking may lead to risky situations such as opening doors and wandering outside. It's important to take precautions if your toddler has this problem. Even if your toddler is still in the crib, they may try to climb out in their sleep, adding to the potential safety issues that surround this phenomenon.

Try this: Rather than trying to wake your sleepwalker up, gently guide him back to his bed or crib. Use baby gates to block stairs and areas of the house you don't want them wandering into. Keep windows and doors locked to prevent your toddler from opening them. Make sure that there are no hard or sharp objects around their sleeping space, and don't put them in beds or cribs that they may fall out of.

Bedwetting

As toddlers are still potty training, chances are high that your toddler's bedwetting is due to not yet having developed sufficient control. However, if you feel that your toddler's bedwetting is pathological, seek advice from your pediatrician. In the meantime, be patient as you help your toddler master a night without wetting the bed.

Try this: Reduce your toddler's fluid intake before bed, and remember to increase it during the day so that they still get enough to drink. Avoid caffeine and citrus juices as these can irritate the bladder. Don't punish your toddler if an accident happens—instead, use positive encouragement and rewards to make them feel good about success. In the event that your toddler simply isn't ready to control their bladder at night, consider letting them wear a pullup to bed even if they've graduated to 'big kid' underwear during the day.

Regression

Another important consideration to take into account as you analyze your baby's sleep is regression. Sometimes, a baby who has learned to fall asleep easily will suddenly begin having trouble dropping off. Other times, babies who have learned to sleep through the night will go back to waking up several times before morning. These types of regressions are normal, and are not necessarily a cause for alarm.

Many baby's go through a regression at around four months and again every four to six months thereafter. However, regression could happen at any time as your baby grows and develops and sleep patterns change. Regressions usually last between one and four weeks and may have no apparent cause.

You may feel frustrated if your baby experiences a regression. For tired parents, times like these can make it seem that all of your hard work to sleep train your baby has gone out the window. Take heart! By training your baby for healthy sleep, you are giving them a solid foundation for development.

Regressions are temporary, so don't stop the training just because your baby seems to have back slid. Continue to engage in the four steps outlined in this book as you and your baby work through the regression together. In a few weeks, things will usually be back on track until the next time.

Chapter 11: Teaching Your Baby the Art of Sleeping

It may seem like a silly notion to an adult who is sleep deprived and hoping for a solid night's rest, but you really need to teach your baby the art of sleeping. You had to learn at some point and now you need to teach your baby. As shocking as it may sound, it isn't always instinct. Sleep is a necessity, but learning the art of sleeping requires a bit of training.

Babies and toddlers are thrust into a big, strange world. They want to explore every inch of it. When they feel the pull of sleep trying to bring them down, it is only natural they would want to fight it in order to keep exploring. They want to stay awake so they can interact with mom, dad and their siblings. They likely feel they are going to miss out on something really spectacular if they give into their body's need for sleep. Haven't you ever stayed up late watching a television show even though you knew you were going to be tired the next day? Of course you have! It is essentially the same thing with little ones. They figure they don't really need all the sleep mom and dad keep insisting on.

You want to teach them that sleeping is a good thing. Making sleep an enjoyable activity will help sway their way of thinking. Although they won't understand solid reasoning like telling them they will feel better after they get a good night's rest, you can persuade them to sleep in their bed by making it a pleasant experience.

Differentiating Between Night and Day

Your first goal is teaching your baby night and day. When you get your baby home from the hospital, you will quickly realize they have no regard for when the household is sleeping and when it is awake. You can start training your baby in the first few days of life. Here's how it works:

1-Place your baby's bed near a window. Do your best to get up at the same time every day. If it is 5 am or 8 am, stick with it. If the baby is sleeping, open the window to let the light in or turn on the light. This will help baby to see daylight means awake time.

2-At bedtime and naptime, darken the room. Darkness means sleep. Your baby will start to grasp this concept fairly early on if you stick to a routine.

3-During daytime feedings, play with your baby's feet, talk with the baby and keep the lights on. Nighttime feedings will be in low-light, with no playing, talking or giggling. The child will start to learn the difference between the feedings. Nighttime feedings will be shorter and you and the baby will get more sleep.

Rituals and Routines

The first three months of your baby's life are going to be pretty much on his schedule. Although you can start "training" the baby to sleep by nursing, bathing and shutting down the lights as part of the bedtime routine, know that at this young age, the baby needs frequent feedings. Every baby is different, but on average, a child will only go 2 to 4 hours between feedings. Trying to establish a set routine is a little difficult. If you typically go to bed at 9, start your baby's bedtime routine around 8, depending on how long it takes. If you need to bathe, feed, burp and then rock to sleep, you are looking at a good hour. Don't start the process at 9 and become frustrated when the baby doesn't fall asleep until 10.

Experiment early on with various bedtime rituals. A word of caution about lengthy rituals, once you have established a ritual, it will likely carry through the child's early years. If you are not up for a 45-minute ritual every night for the next several years, don't start it now.

No-Cry Method versus Cry it Out

You have likely heard arguments on both sides of the debate. Some experts and well-meaning friends and family members, will tell you to put the baby in bed and let him cry until he eventually falls asleep. Others will tell you leaving your baby alone and crying is a betrayal and your baby will not learn to distrust you. Both sides have valid arguments. What it comes down to is what feels right to you. Are you okay leaving your baby to cry for 15 to 30 minutes? If not, don't feel as if you are "spoiling" your baby if you can't do it. However, you will want to give your baby a chance to soothe himself. Here are some tips that are in line with both methods:

- When the baby is crying, leave him in bed, but gently rub his tummy or stand next to the crib while singing or humming.
- When the baby cries, pick him up, soothe him and put him right back in bed.
- Establish key sounds/words like "shhh" or "sleepy time" to soothe the child into sleep.
- Stand outside the door or put a chair outside the door of baby's room, when he starts crying, talk to him from the door, but don't go in the room.

Your baby is of course going to be comforted by the sound of your voice and being able to be close to you. It isn't surprising that some babies are a little hesitant to fall asleep if they know they will be separated from their parents. You want the baby to know sleeping is safe and you will be there to take care of their needs no matter what. Soothing the baby when he is in bed will help him understand he isn't alone or abandoned.

It will take some time for the baby to learn sleeping is a wonderful thing. Parents will need to have patience and realize that training a baby to sleep has its ups and downs, but it will happen eventually. The key is learning your baby's personality and what works. Once you have discovered what works best for your baby, it is all about consistency. Allow yourself a minimum of a full week of following a consistent routine to train your baby how to sleep. Don't give up on the second or third night because it isn't working. You need to give it some time before you move on to the next method.

You can help your child feel tired and ready to welcome sleep by keeping him busy during his awake time. When the weather allows, get the child outside to explore his new world. Babies who crawl or walk will love running just to run. You don't want to over-stimulate the child, but you want the child to get all of his exploring done during his waking hours. For infants and newborns, tummy time, feeding and spending time chatting with mom and dad is plenty of stimulation. Look for signs the child is wearing down and start on the bedtime routine. If it is 20 minutes earlier than usual, that is okay. Your baby will do best when he is put to sleep when he is tired and not over tired.

Common sleepy signs include:

- Yawning
- Slowing down - crawlers may prefer to just lay on the floor while walkers will sit down
- Rubbing the eyes
- Fussiness
- Breast fed baby may "root" when being held

Do your best to watch for the signs. You want to put the baby to bed when he is still awake, but on the verge of falling asleep. It will make your job much easier and will help teach the child he can fall asleep on his own.

Naps—Good or Bad

You have probably heard the reasoning you need to keep the baby awake during the day so he will sleep through the night. No naps would mean the baby is so exhausted by bedtime he will fall right to sleep and not wake up until the next morning, right? WRONG!

We have already discussed the importance of sleep for your child. A child is not physically capable of sleeping 12 hours straight. Their little tummies need food more often than an adult. Depriving your child of a nap or two during the day is doing nothing but making your life more difficult and making the child cranky. You absolutely must do what you can to get your baby to nap during the day.

Without adequate sleep, your child will struggle to go to sleep at night. When he does fall asleep, it will likely be a restless sleep that will keep you up anyway. Babies need plenty of sleep in order to be healthy and develop properly. By reasoning the baby will be so tired he will just pass out will backfire! A child who is overtired will lack the coping mechanisms needed to soothe himself to sleep.

Newborn to 6 months

Your newborn will likely sleep off and on throughout the night and day. Setting up established nap times is very difficult at this age because the child is growing and his needs are changing. Your baby will only be awake for 4 to 8 hours during the entire 24-hour period. Ideally, you would prefer those waking hours to be during the day, but it doesn't always happen that way. Do your best to put your baby down for several naps throughout the day to keep him rested and more able to handle longer sleeping periods at night.

6 months to a 1 year

At this stage, your baby's feeding needs are not quite as demanding. You can expect the child to start sleeping for longer blocks of time at night, which means more awake time during the day. A typical schedule for a child of this age is bed at 8 and awake at 6 with two naps during the day. Expect the naps to last about 2 hours each. The first nap may be at 10 a.m.. The baby wakes up eats lunch and plays for a few hours before another nap around 3 or 4. The baby will sleep a couple of hours, wake up, eat dinner, play and be ready for bedtime.

1 to 3 years

Babies at this age are typically able to sleep through the night and will likely only need one nap during the day. Nap times vary, but average anywhere from one to three hours. The nap should be timed so it is about halfway through the baby's waking hours. After lunch is a good time depending on what the child's schedule is.

3 to 5 years

Each child will differ in the amount of sleep they need. There are plenty of preschoolers who will do just fine without a nap, while others absolutely must have one. The child's nap needs will typically depend on the quality of sleep they are getting at night. You will need to watch the child and look for signs of sleepiness. If the child is tired, put him down for a nap. It may not be needed every day. It is important a child does not become overly tired. If you have had a busy day running at the park for hours, the child will likely be tired and need a nap to get through the rest of the day. Use your best judgment.

Overall, naps are absolutely necessary not only for the child's health and development, but for your own mental health. Taking care of babies and toddlers is a big job. You cannot leave them alone for a minute and have to be on high alert all the time. Nap time gives you some time to relax or even catch a little sleep yourself.

The trick is timing the naps for your baby or toddler so they don't interfere with the long block of nighttime sleep. Your child will need anywhere from 2 to 4 hours to wind down after waking from a nap. If your scheduled bedtime is at 8, naptime should be over by 4 or 5 at the latest. It can take several weeks before you figure out the right routine for your child. The child may fight naps every day, every single nap, but as long as you are persistent and consistent, they will realize there is no escaping the nap.

You will likely need to employ some of the sleep solutions mentioned throughout this book. Darken the room, put on some quiet music, rock the child or whatever has become part of the sleep routine to help them understand that it is time to rest for a bit.

Chapter 12: Safety

There are several aspects to putting your baby to bed safely, and many of them will be included below. While guidelines and other advice may be based on scientific findings, many people manage to ignore them and continue on to have a happy, healthy baby. For many others, though, what is the point in taking that risk? If you can minimize any risk to your baby, shouldn't you do so? For instance, there are some parents who have an issue with the idea that they cannot decorate their baby's crib. Many doctors have said that if you want to decorate something, decorate the baby's room. Your baby's crib is designed to be a safety device. Use it that way.

By eliminating things that could become loose and cause an issue for a baby who lacks full motor skills, you are ensuring that these things will not be a problem. How can you worry about a giant stuffed bear with a ribbon possibly smothering your child in the crib if it is not there? No errant strings can cause an issue from a blanket that is not in the crib. Or if you are worried about your baby remaining warm throughout the night, there is a ton of adorable options available from sleep sacks to footed pajamas.

The American Academy of Pediatrics has successfully cut the rate of crib death, also known as SIDS, down by a staggering 50% by implementing a few guidelines. While most parents have heard these statistics and facts, it is important to stay up to date as there is always going to be improvements and adjustments made. For example, the minimization of the amount of space between crib slats eliminated the need for baby bumpers, which cut down on two causes of infant death.

Thankfully, after these points were made, many babies and their parents no longer had the concern of the baby getting their head stuck in the sides of the crib. Further, the removal of the bumpers eliminated the possibility of suffocation. And the elimination of cribs with drop-down sides has also improved the statistics of babies injured while in their beds or the older toddlers who have learned to climb out.

In the interest of the welfare of all of our precious babies, here are the guidelines for putting babies to bed safely. Some of them may not seem directly related, but we all know how important our children are. Let's keep them safe any way we can. At the top of the list of tips to decrease the risk of SIDS for your baby is breastfeeding. According to a study that was published in the June 2011 issue of Pediatrics, children who were exclusively breastfed had over a 50% decreased risk of SIDS. There are many different speculations as to why this is, including the number of antibodies that breastfed babies receive. It has also been noted in speculation that breastfed babies are easier to awaken, which is a very significant point as babies who have difficulties being woken up have been found to be more prone to SIDS.

For the many mothers who may be on a particular medication that does not allow for them to breastfeed, do not be discouraged. There are plenty of additional measures you can take to ensure you reduce your baby's risk as much as possible. Adherence to vaccination schedules is also highly emphasized since research published in 2007 in the Vaccine journal showed that infants who were properly immunized also had a nearly 50% lower chance of SIDS. Surprisingly, pacifiers have also been linked to reducing the risk of SIDS. Appropriate pacifiers can be used at nap time and bedtime.

Additional guidelines include laying your baby in a sturdy, firm crib covered only with a fitted sheet; no blankets, pillows, or stuffed animals should be in the crib. Why? By eliminating pillows, there are no allergens or loose threads, and the baby's head will not sink into it. Without things in the crib, you will have a clear view of your baby with the baby monitor. And as your baby gets older and the twitches turn to fidgeting or playing with their fingers, you do not have to worry about them possibly wrapping something around their head or their limbs and cutting off circulation. Also, it is better to avoid the use of foam wedges and sleep positioners.

Babies should be laid down to sleep on their backs every time they go to sleep. Now, you may be concerned about a flattened head (also known as positional plagiocephaly) due to your baby spending so much of the day in this position. If this concerns you, consider using supervised tummy time to keep them awake and engaged during the daytime, which will help enforce your sleep schedule and allow you to bond with your baby. While some babies love to be swaddled and sleep very well that way, not every baby is a fan. For those babies who like to fidget, a sleep sack can be a cute and cozy alternative to a blanket. A footed pajama is also a good choice. For those whose babies love being swaddled but cannot quite get the snug, secure wrapping correct right away, there are plenty of swaddling blankets available.

Safety is a very important factor to ensure that both you and your baby have a good night's sleep. Let's talk about a few of the important factors that will contribute to your baby's safety when it comes to sleeping.

•	Sleeping Position – It is important that newborns sleep on their back. Recent studies have shown that babies who sleep on their backs rather than their tummies have a lower risk of SIDS.

As babies grow older and learn to roll over, many babies will roll around and sleep on their sides or even on their tummies. Once they can roll around on their own, doctors and pediatricians say that you do not have to worry about how they sleep, but you should still always put them to bed on their backs. If they then roll over, that's fine.

•	Firm Sleeping Surface – It is extremely important that your baby has a firm surface to sleep on in order to avoid suffocation. Suffocation can happen easily if you allow your baby to fall asleep in his car seat for long periods of time like overnight. Obviously he'll sleep in his car seat when you are out driving around town, and that's okay, but you never want to let his car seat replace his crib or mattress. It is too easy for his head to fall forward, cutting off the air flow through his windpipe. Even if he falls asleep in the car while driving, you should be checking on him often to make sure that this does not happen.

•	Remove All Loose Objects from the Crib – Especially as your newborn becomes a little more mobile in her crib, you'll want to make sure there are no loose objects in the crib that she could pull over her face or could roll into, causing her to suffocate during the night. Sometimes a baby rolls and then doesn't realize the need to roll away or can't figure out how to roll again. A stuffed animal, extra blanket, etc. could all be dangerous objects of concern for your newborn in this situation.

• Do Not Cover Your Baby's Head – Perhaps this goes without saying, but even placing an extra blanket around your baby's head to keep him warm may get pulled over his head throughout the course of the night. Even young babies will move their arms and legs some and can get tangled in things if they are too close to their head. If that happens and the extra blanket gets pulled up and over his head, it could possibly suffocate him or even overheat him. It is vital that you think ahead about all the possibilities when doing anything with your newborn.

• Implement Tummy Time – Simply lay your baby down on the carpet and on her tummy during the day and keep a close eye on her. Tummy time allows your baby to start developing the muscles in her neck and arms that will help her roll around and away from things. This helps her immensely with her safety since when she gets into a dangerous situation, she now has the ability to roll in the opposite direction.

Often when little ones get themselves too close to a blanket or stuffed animal, they know they want to roll away, but they don't know how. They have the survival instincts to know the situation is bad, but they don't know what to do. By helping them develop the muscles to roll around through tummy time, they learn quickly how to navigate effectively around their cribs.

Helping your baby sleep through the night is also about ensuring that your baby is safe while in her crib. When you put her to bed, make sure that everything around her is safe and comfortable, and you will be able to sleep better knowing that she is in a safe place for the night.

It will still be hard for the first little while not to go running in there to check on her and make sure that she is still breathing after a few hours, but eventually you'll be happy that she is sleeping, and you'll enjoy the quiet of the night knowing that she is safe and that you are doing what is best for the both of you.

Conclusion

We all need to get quality sleep. Babies need to sleep so that their physical and brain health will properly develop and we adults need sleep so that our bodies can restore and rejuvenate.

It is true, that when you become a parent, getting quality sleep may seem almost impossible, as if sleep deprivation is a typical part of life. However, this does not have to remain true forever.

Many parents, my husband and I included, were able to get some good shut-eye through sleep training our babies— which benefitted not only our little one, but us as well.

I hope that you will use the tips and methods that you learned in this book as you coach your child to sleep. No, it will not be an easy feat, but you will get there through patience and commitment.

What's a few months of "hard" work when the result is many good nights of sleep for you and your baby?

You can do it, mom and dad!

Lastly, if you enjoyed this audiobook I ask that you please take the time to review it on Audible.com. Your honest feedback would be greatly appreciated.

Thank you.

www.ingramcontent.com/pod-product-compliance
Lightning Source LLC
Chambersburg PA
CBHW021128080526
44587CB00012B/1190